T0150425

THE
LITTLE
BOOK
OF
EDINBURGH

GEOFF HOLDER

The
History
Press

To the Auld Alliance, although perhaps
not the one you're thinking of. *Allons-y!*

First published 2013
Reprinted 2015
This paperback edition published 2020

The History Press
97 St George's Place
Cheltenham, Glos
GL50 3QB
www.thehistorypress.co.uk

British Library Cataloguing in Publication Data.
A catalogue record for this book is available from the British Library.

ISBN 978 0 7509 9399 9
Typesetting and origination by The History Press
Printed in Great Britain by TJ Books Limited

CONTENTS

ACKNOWLEDGEMENTS

As well as the usual writer's support network (you know who you are), thanks go out to the library angels of Edinburgh Central Library and its Edinburgh and Scottish Collection; the National Library of Scotland; and the A.K. Bell Library, Perth. I'd also like to express my gratitude to the staff of all the museums, galleries, visitor attractions and cafés I visited in the course of researching this book. Oh, the suffering.

The topographical views are taken from *Modern Athens, or Edinburgh in the Nineteenth Century* by Thomas H. Shepherd (1829-1831). All other illustrations are from various Victorian and Edwardian volumes of *Punch*, with the exception of the images of Burke and Hare, which are courtesy of Cate Ludlow.

INTRODUCTION

'The most beautiful of all the capitols of Europe.'
Sir John Betjeman, *First and Last Loves* (1952)

'This accursed, stinking, reeky mass of stones and lime and dung.'
Thomas Carlyle, letter to his brother (1821)

These two quotes perfectly sum up Edinburgh. It *is* spectacularly beautiful, combining a dramatic natural landscape of hills, valleys and the cone of an extinct volcano with an architectural heritage so glorious that it has more listed buildings than anywhere in the UK outside London. And at the same time there *is* a grimness to the place, a secret, gritty history of dark deeds and squalor. It is this combination – beauty and the beast, if you like – that makes Edinburgh so utterly fascinating, so beguiling.

One of Edinburgh's most famous sons, Robert Louis Stevenson, knew this better than anyone. His novel *Dr Jekyll and Mr Hyde*, about two conflicting personalities inhabiting the same body, is a virtual metaphor for his native city. Edinburgh is a 'tale of two cities', or rather, many different tales. Historically, there are the two cities: the Old Town, a medieval gloom-a-thon of narrow lanes, twisting streets and hunchbacked buildings; and the New Town, an Enlightenment vision of wide, straight streets, elegant crescents and neo-Classical mansions. Take it further, and you literally have two cities – the City of Edinburgh and the Port of Leith, neighbours only formally joined as late as 1920, and still bearing a sense of difference.

Socially, there is the gulf between the intellectual, moneyed and professional classes – who, since the sixteenth century, have made up a major segment of the population – and those at the lower end of the social scale. When Charles Dickens visited, he found the highest levels of sophistication and civilisation operating just a few streets away from scenes of poverty worse than he had found in the East End of London. Today, St Andrew Square and Charlotte Square in the New Town are the most expensive pieces of real estate in Scotland, while

some of the peripheral housing estates are wastelands of drugs and gang violence.

How about the duality of hypocrisy? In the early 1800s some of the finest minds in Europe were pushing forward the frontiers of knowledge on the one hand – and on the other condoning grave robbing and even murder. A few decades earlier, Deacon Brodie, town councillor and respectable businessman by day, was, under the cover of darkness, a master burglar and thief.

Even physically, Edinburgh has two parts: up and down. Streets that appear to be adjacent when looking on the map are in fact separated by great cliffs of buildings that can only be negotiated by prodigious stairwells. A street-level shop on one road turns out to be one of the upper storeys of a tenement that has its roots in the urban valley far below. Edinburgh, the precipitous city, is as full of hills and glens as any heather-clad country district, even if the topography is camouflaged by brick and stone.

There is another dichotomy to savour. Not that long ago, Edinburgh was the city of disapproval and distaste, where fun was forbidden and pleasure proscribed. These days it is one of the most enjoyable small cities on the planet, where there is always too much to see and too little time to do everything. It is a city dedicated to culture and excitement, a feast for the mind and the senses. Whether it is delving into the myriad delights of the Festival, or marvelling at the treasures in a museum or gallery, or simply pounding the streets in search of architectural wonders and then settling into a back street café, your experience of Edinburgh is guaranteed to be extraordinary.

And it's that extraordinariness that has inspired this book. There is history, but this is not a history of the city. There is culture, but this is not a guidebook. There is sport, and the natural world, and the world of work and play, and war and heroism and crime and police. This is a canter through the intriguing, bizarre and wonderful story of this most Jekyll and Hyde of cities.

The feeling grows upon you that this also is a piece of nature in the most intimate sense; this profusion of eccentricities, this dream in masonry and living rock is not a drop scene in a theatre, but a city in the world of every-day reality.

Robert Louis Stevenson, *Edinburgh: Picturesque Notes* (1878)

1

PLACES –
HERE & NOW,
THEN & THERE

PREHISTORIC DAYS

Edinburgh has the earliest known human settlement in Scotland. Analysis of hazelnut shells found in the temporary camp occupied by Mesolithic hunter-gatherers at Cramond has produced a date of 8,500 BC, when ice covered much of the country.

Edinburgh also has one of Scotland's earliest permanent dwellings – a Neolithic roundhouse at Ravelrig Hill near Dalmahoy. The early farm was established about 3,000 BC, roughly the same time as the famous settlement of Skara Brae in Orkney.

A Bronze Age tribe occupied Castle Rock in 900 BC, the first of many peoples who recognised the hill's defensive position.

WHAT DID THE ROMANS EVER DO FOR US?

Cramond had a Roman fort and harbour. The site produced the sculpture of a lioness eating a man, one of the finest pieces of Roman art found in Britain. The outline of the fort can still be seen beside Cramond Church and the sculpture is in the National Museum of Scotland on Chambers Street.

The National Museum also has a fantastic collection of silver objects discovered on Traprain Law, a volcanic hill in East Lothian. The treasure seems to have been payment from the Romans to one of their client tribes, the Votadini, who also occupied Edinburgh's Castle Rock. The Votadini had chosen not to resist the invasion and as a result prospered through trade with Rome. After the Romans left, the powerful Votadins, now called the Gododdins, established a kingdom based on their timber fortress on Castle Rock.

WHAT'S IN A NAME?

No one really knows the origins of the city's name. The best evidence suggests that Dun Eidyn or Din Eidyn was the name given to Castle Rock by the Kingdom of Gododdin, 'Dun' meaning fort. The Gododdin were Celtic Britons; in the seventh century, when the area was occupied by the Angles (whose language later mutated into English and Scots), the name lost the 'dun' element and gained the '–burgh' suffix, from the Old English word 'burh' (fort). Medieval versions of the name include Edenesburch, Edynburgh and Edynburghe, and even in the seventeenth century you could read of Edenborough, Edenborrow or Edenburgh.

Modern scholars reject the once-popular notion that 'Edinburgh' is derived from 'Edwinesburh' (Edwin's fort), a supposed reference to Edwin, a seventh-century king of the Angles. The Scottish Gaelic version of the name, *Dùn Éideann*, is a transliteration of 'Dun Eidyn', and has led some people to call the city Dunedin.

Vernacular variants include Embra and Embro, and poets have used the term Edina, while the coal-hungry and be-chimneyed city has been known as Auld Reekie (Scots for Old Smoky) since the seventeenth century.

MEDIEVAL EDINBURGH

Edinburgh was a walled city from the late Middle Ages onwards. The King's Wall, built in 1450, excluded the low-lying Grassmarket, even though the open space, along with the Cowgate, was already an established part of the city.

The larger Flodden Wall, erected in a panic in 1513 after the catastrophic Battle of Flodden to keep the English out (they didn't come), was more generous, extending further to the south. Fragments of the Flodden Wall can be seen today on Keir Street and in Greyfriars Kirkyard.

For 250 years no one built outside the confines of the Flodden Wall. The population, however, kept rising. The only solution was to build upwards, creating the world's first skyscrapers, 'lands' that at their extreme could count fourteen floors from the lower level of the back lanes on the slope to the wind-blasted upper garret.

In 1636 almost all of the city's 60,000 inhabitants were living in the Royal Mile and its sixty attendant closes and wynds. The overcrowding was fearsome, akin to a shanty-town or refugee camp of today.

The Protestant Reformation of the sixteenth century destroyed a treasury of church items deemed 'idolatrous', such as statues, woodcarvings and stained glass. The only complete stained-glass windows remaining from medieval Scotland can be found in the Magdellan Chapel on Cowgate.

The principal entry through the Flodden Wall was Netherbow Port, which stood at the Royal Mile junction of Jeffrey Street and St Mary's Street, at the head of Canongate. For many years this marked the boundary of the city of Edinburgh (Canongate was in another jurisdiction), and so the area became known as World's End. The old world of medieval thinking did end after the failed Jacobite Rebellion of 1745-46, and, with armed attack no longer a threat, the Port was demolished in 1764. Brass plaques in the roadway now mark the site of the Port.

The Royal Mile derives its name from the route that stretches from the fortress of Edinburgh Castle (defender of the kingdom and home of the Scottish Regalia) down the slope to Holyrood Palace (constructed in the early sixteenth century as the royal residence in Edinburgh). It is approximately 1 old Scots mile long, about 12 per cent longer than a current statute mile.

NAVAL GAZING

In the fifteenth century the *Yellow Caravel*, an armed merchant ship belonging to the privateer Sir Andrew Wood of Largo, stranded on a sandbank at the entrance to the port of Leith. As Wood's two ships were effectively the extent of Scotland's (semi-private) navy at the time, this lack of safe passage was a major issue. James IV therefore had the tiny fishing harbour of St Mary's Port, just along the coast, built up into a full-scale facility called New Haven Port of Grace (now Newhaven). Leith's later docks expansion has obscured the once important role Newhaven played in medieval Scotland.

The year 1511 saw the initial launch of the *Great Michael*, a huge four-masted man-o'-war or carrack, the pride of James IV's nascent Royal Scottish Navy. To build the ship and its dock, Newhaven had become Scotland's premier industrial centre, employing hundreds, and consuming huge swathes of timber (including, it is said, most of the forests in Fife, and all the trees lining the Water of Leith).

Building the *Great Michael* was the equivalent of constructing the largest aircraft carrier of modern days, and then some. She was the largest warship in Europe at the time. After years of work the carrack finally took up station in early 1513, riding at anchor in the Firth of Forth in the lee of the island of Inchkeith, ready to take on any English raiders. No such conflict occurred. A few months later, James IV was killed at the Battle of Flodden, and a crisis-ridden Scotland sold the hugely costly ship to France at a knockdown price.

CITY OF SEVEN HILLS?

At some point in the eighteenth century, which was obsessed with the Classical world, it became standard practice to refer to Edinburgh as built on seven hills, in the same manner as Rome. Edinburgh certainly has many steep gradients, as pedestrians and cyclists quickly discover. But are there really only seven hills?

The annual Seven Hills of Edinburgh race takes the traditional view. Its seven are:

Calton Hill, just east of the New Town.
Castle Rock.
Corstorphine Hill in the west of the city.
Craiglockhart Hill, Braid Hill and Blackford Hill, all in the south.
Arthur's Seat, to the east.

Other hills not on this list can be found in the New Town, Dalry, Sighthill and Fairmilehead, most of which are not noticed because they are built over. Fairmilehead, however, at 183m high, is higher than four hills on the traditional list.

The highest point within the city boundaries is Arthur's Seat. The Pentland Hills just to the south of the city are far higher, but it is Arthur's Seat's elevation of 251m that dominates the skyline and helps to provide Edinburgh's distinctive profile.

OPINIONS ON A GRAND CITY

In 1435 an Italian nobleman arrived on a secret mission to meet King James I, a visit so sensitive that, to his great discomfort, Aeneas Sylvius Piccolomini was forced to travel by ship all the way to Scotland rather than risk being taken by the English. After being storm-tossed and being rendered permanently lame by frostbite arthritis through walking on snow-covered roads, Aeneas found Scotland somewhat uncongenial, and noted in his autobiography, *The Commentaries*, 'There is nothing the Scotch like better to hear than abuse of the English.' The pretty women of Edinburgh and environs, however, were a different matter, and the dashing Italian fathered a child during his visit. Twenty-three years later, Aeneas Sylvius Piccolomini became Pope Pius.

The pre-Papal visit is recorded in a beautiful fresco within the grandiose Piccolomin Library in Siena, Tuscany. The 'Oration as envoy before King James I of Scotland', created by the Renaissance artist Pinturicchio in the first decade of the sixteenth century, shows King James and his court gathered in a sunny Italian portico surrounded by luscious foliage. In reality the meeting took place in the depths of winter in a place Aeneas described thus: 'A cold country where few things will grow and for the most part it has no trees.'

Throw a stone anywhere in Edinburgh today and you will be in danger of breaking the windows of several hotels, bed and breakfasts, youth hostels and other accommodations for the travel-weary visitor. In the eighteenth century, however, the situation was very different. In 1774 Captain Edward Topham wrote to a friend that, 'There is no inn that is better than an ale-house, nor any accommodation that is decent, cleanly or fit to receive a gentleman.' Stopping at what was reputed to be the best inn in the city, Topham was dismayed to discover that he was expected to share bedding with another eight or ten people. He found alternative lodgings on the High Street, which he however said were 'so infernal in appearance' that he could have been in a particularly dirty Hell.

'The city is placed in a dainty, healthful and pure air and doubtless was a most healthful place to live in,' wrote Sir William Brereton in 1634. The English visitor gloried in the architecture and setting of Edinburgh, but he was less than impressed by the eye-watering, nose-holding stench, adding, 'were not the inhabitants most sluttish, nasty and slothful people.'

The much-mocked nineteenth-century poet William McGonagall, in describing the Grassmarket, quoted Mark Twain's opinion on an Italian city: 'The streets are narrow and the smells are abominable, yet, on reflection, I am glad to say they are narrow – if they had been wider they would have held more smell, and killed all the people.'

Virtually every eighteenth and nineteenth-century visitor to Edinburgh remarked on the city's awful smell. Given that many of these visitors came from London or Glasgow, themselves places hardly gentle on the nose, Edinburgh must have truly stunk to high heaven.

Georgian Edinburgh was, however, widely recognised for the quality of its intellectual life. 'Here stand I,' said Mr Amyat, a London visitor, 'at what is called the Cross of Edinburgh, and can in a few minutes take fifty men of genius by the hand.'

Others have been less kind. The religious fanatic and Covenanter Patrick Walker denounced the city as: 'Sinful Edinburgh, the Sink of Abominations, that has defiled the whole Land, where Satan sometime a Day had his seat.'

EDINBURGH'S CASTLES

Edinburgh Castle on Castle Rock is one of the most famous fortifications in the world, and the city's Number One tourist attraction. There are, however, a number of less famous castles dotted around the city.

Merchiston Castle or Tower sits amidst Napier University's Merchiston campus. Built around 1454, the tower was damaged in 1572 during the war between rival supporters of Mary, Queen of Scots and her son, the future James VI. Restoration work in the 1960s uncovered a 26-pound cannonball embedded in the tower wall.

Napier University has a second castle, although the tower house of Craiglockhart Castle on Craiglockhart campus is quite ruinous.

Liberton Tower in the suburb of the same name is a fairly plain tower house in good condition.

Cramond Tower, a restored seventeenth-century tower house in Cramond village, is a private residence, as is Barnbougle Castle west of Cramond. Barnbougle's medieval structure was entirely rebuilt in Scots Baronial style in 1881.

Bavelaw Castle is another restored structure in private hands, this one southwest of the city.

Lauriston Castle, between Cramond and Davidson's Mains, is open to the public, and has lovely grounds.

The much-altered Craigcrook Castle in Blackhall mostly dates from the seventeenth century, and in later times hosted a variety of literary luminaries from Charles Dickens to Hans Christian Anderson. It is currently occupied by several businesses.

Lennox Tower near Currie is very badly ruined, a mere shadow of its former self.

The huge medieval Craigmillar Castle is where the plot was hatched to murder Lord Darnley, the husband of Mary, Queen of Scots. A true labyrinth of a castle – very much worth a visit – a skeleton was found walled up in the dungeon here.

LOST CASTLES

No matter how many castles currently populate Edinburgh, even more have vanished.

Red Hall Tower in Slateford was destroyed by Oliver Cromwell's army in 1650, and replaced by the more comfortable mansion of Redhall House a little over a century later.

The only reminder of Curriehill Castle is the road named after it, Curriehill Castle Drive.

Malleny Castle in Balerno had already vanished by the late eighteenth century.

Vague traces of an unknown fourteenth-century stronghold have been found at Broomhall Terrace in South Gyle.

Inchgarvie Castle was a sixteenth-century tower on the island of Inchgarvie in the Forth. Its few remains were incorporated into the gun battery built on the island during the Napoleonic Wars, and then again into the anti-aircraft battery of the Second World War.

Fifteenth-century Mortonhall Castle near the present Mortonhall had a moat and drawbridge, but not a stone or ridge survives of the site.

The ruinous but impressive Granton Castle (aka Royston House) on West Shore Road was demolished after the First World War down to the foundations and beyond.

The presence of the medieval castle of Corstorphine is marked only by its doocot (pigeon house) off Dovecot Road. The doocot is in good condition: the occupants of its 1,060 nest boxes provided valuable meat and fertilizer.

The castellated Georgian mansion of Dreghorn Castle near the bypass was demolished as late as 1955.

Leith has had several fortifications, although you would hardly know it today. The earliest, the vast earthen ramparts erected in 1560 when the Catholic French in the port were besieged by the Scottish and English Protestants, have vanished, although two of the gun platforms built by the besiegers can still be seen on Leith Links.

The fragments of Leith Citadel, built by Oliver Cromwell in the 1650s, can be glimpsed at the northern end of Leith Walk.

In 1779 the Scot-turned-American privateer John Paul Jones sailed into the Firth of Forth intent on attacking British shipping and ports in support of the American War of Independence. He was pushed out to sea by a gale. A small part of the wall and guardhouses still survives of the hurriedly-constructed Leith Fort from this time.

Perhaps Edinburgh's most comprehensively vanished castle is Dingwall Castle, built in the 1520s on the site of what is now Waverley Station. After a brief life as a courtyard castle and then re-use as a prison, it was robbed for building materials in the 1640s and had disappeared long before the New Town development and the arrival of the railways. Most histories of the city never mention it.

PLACE-NAME PECULIARITIES

Holy Corner, the crossroads of Morningside Road, Chamberlain Road and Colinton Road, is so named because four churches dominate the site.

Irish Corner, meanwhile, was the name given to the junction between Saughton Street and Corstorphine High Street, because of the immigrants who lived there.

The Lawnmarket on the Royal Mile had nothing to do with gardens. The name means Landmarket, that is, the place where the landward, or country people, held a market.

The Grassmarket was once the Sheep Flechts, reflecting its function as a livestock market.

A quaint legend supposedly explains the name of Morocco Land on Canongate. Andrew Grey fled a sentence of death in Edinburgh and ended up in North Africa. After twelve years in exile, and now immensely wealthy, he returned, bent on revenge. However, in a change of plan, he ended up marrying the Provost's daughter (after first curing her of the plague). Having taken a vow never to set foot in Edinburgh, he settled in Canongate – which was technically outside the city boundaries – and set up a statue of the emperor of Morocco on his house. You can choose to believe as much of this tale as you wish.

Dean Bridge, designed by Thomas Telford, opened in 1832 to link the New Town with the routes to the west. It soon became known as the Bridge of Sighs – because so many people committed suicide by jumping into the Water of Leith 108ft below. The parapet was eventually raised in an attempt to inhibit the jumpers.

By the 1980s the twenty-storey Thomas Fraser Court off North Junction Street in Leith was suffering the social decline common to many tower blocks. As part of the regeneration of the block, it was refurbished and given a suitably upbeat new name – Persevere Court.

The curved structure of Cable Wynd House in Leith meant, inevitably, it was nicknamed Banana Block.

The local pronunciation of Admiralty Street in Leith is 'Admirality Street', with an extra 'i'. Antigua and Montague Streets were pronounced 'Antaygi' and 'Montaygi' respectively.

A native of Newhaven is known as a Bow Tow.

Wester Hailes Road was originally known as Thieves Road.

The steps leading from Saxe Coburg Street to Glenogle Road were called, with striking insensitivity, the Dummy Steps, because the Deaf and Dumb School was nearby.

The standard explanation for the name of the suburb of Liberton is that it is a corruption of 'lipper's town' or Leper Town, there having supposedly been a leprosy hospital here. However, no trace of such a refuge has been found, and the name Liberton predates the appearance of leprosy in Scotland.

Probably the most disputed placename is Arthur's Seat. Some people are convinced it refers to King Arthur. Others think it commemorates an entirely different Prince Arthur from the Dark Ages. An idea popular in the nineteenth century was that the name was a corruption of 'Archers Seat', on the assumption that bowmen had been based on the commanding height during some medieval battle. The most likely provenance is that 'Arthur's Seat' is a mangled version of a Gaelic placename.

SOME UNUSUAL STREET NAMES

Now-demolished Plainstone's Close at 222 Canongate was once known as both Bloody Mary's Close and Bonnie Mary's Close.

Ewerland in Braehead comes from 'ewer', the old word for a basin or jug. The owners of the land, it is said, had been granted the property after saving the life of the king. The only rent they had to pay was to supply the monarch with a ewer of water whenever he rode by. The king's saviour was supposedly named Jock Howieson, and the site of his alleged cottage is nearby by old Cramond Brig, but the story cannot be authenticated, and is very probably fanciful.

Buckstone Loan and its associated streets north of Fairmilehead are named for the Buckstone or Buckstane, where, according to a charter from the early seventeenth century, the laird of Penicuik was required to thrice blow a horn each time the king unleashed his buckhounds to hunt on the Boroughmuir. In a bizarre addition to this feudal holdover, the laird's wife was also duty bound to blow the horn, but only once. Having been moved about a hundred yards, the 3ft-high Buckstane now stands next to a wall opposite the Morton Hall Golf Clubhouse.

Edinburgh has ten Colonies. These are not overseas possessions, but streets of 'model' working-class housing built to a higher standard than was usual in Victorian cities. The Colonies are found in Abbeyhill, Dalry, Fountainbridge, Leith Links, Lochend Road, North Fort Street in Leith, Pilrig, Shandon, Slateford and Stockbridge. Of these the last named are by far the best known, and the attractive 'B'-listed two-storey dwellings are now well beyond most working-class pockets.

Coffin Lane suitably runs to Dalry Cemetery. The Gallolee or Gallows-lea, one of the various sites of execution, could once be found halfway between Edinburgh and Leith. It is not clear what the connection is with The Gallolee on the opposite side of the city in Dreghorn.

Lapicide Place in Newhaven refers not to rabbit-killing but the process of stonecutting.

Fishwives' Causeway in Portobello is another functional streetname, referring to the route taken by the women of the fisher community to the railway station.

Stockbridge is apparently so called because it was where a wooden or 'stock' bridge crossed the Water of Leith.

An Old Testament concentration can be found in Morningside, with Canaan Lane, Jordan Lane, Eden Lane, Nile Grove and Egypt Mews. Joppa Grove in Portobello refers to a place on the coast of the Holy Land.

Beulah in Musselburgh is another Biblical name, meaning the land of Israel, although in English literature, as in John Bunyan's *Pilgrim's Progress*, it has come to signify a place of mystical peace, a 'Shangri-La'.

Pape's Cottages overlooking the Water of Leith are nothing to do with the Papacy; they were built as accommodation for poor widows, as specified in the will of George Pape.

The lane known as John Knox Way was so named on a request from the Orange Lodge in 1971.

Christian Crescent is not a religious appellation: it was named for a Major Christian, Provost of Portobello.

When much of the uncultivated land on the edge of the city was dangerous marsh, a beacon light used to be lit at night on the east gable end of Corstorphine Church, so that travellers could find their way safely. The lamp was funded from the income of an acre of land; and so we have Lampacre Road. The niche continues to have a lamp, installed by the local Rotary Club in 1958.

A slightly less believable story is attached to St Katherine's Gardens. Katherine or Catherine was one of the great martyrs of the early Church, whose story is entirely legendary. Oil that streamed from her uncorrupted body on Mount Sinai supposedly had healing powers; and a few drops of this oil was, according to the story, brought back to Edinburgh and deposited in a well here. The well water was a balm for various diseases, and so we have Balmwell Avenue.

Romance and passion are well served with Tryst Park, Lovers Lane and Wanton Walls.

East Lilypot in Granton seems to have been derived from a now-vanished old house called Lilyput or Lilliput, a reference to *Gulliver's Travels*.

Picardy Place was named after refugee silk workers, who arrived from the Picardy area of northern France in 1730.

Cockmylane in the south of the city, like so many streets that suggest an intriguing story hidden in the name, is probably merely a corruption of a Gaelic original, in this case *cuach na leanaidh*, 'the springs in the hollow of the sloping meadow'. Other examples are Cowpits, which has nothing to do with slaughterhouses as it is a corruption of *pettan cuith*, 'the small farm at a fold'; Galachlaw Shot (*gealachlamh*, 'white hill'); and Fair-a-far, 'hill of the cultivated land'.

There are no street names in Edinburgh beginning with the letter X.

Only one street begins with Z – Zetland Place.

LISTED BUILDINGS

Edinburgh is a mecca for lovers of beautiful buildings and cityscapes. The medieval Old Town and the Georgian New Town were together designated as a UNESCO World Heritage Site in 1995.

There are an astonishing 4,847 listed buildings in Edinburgh. Of these, 909 are Category 'A' listed, meaning they are of national or international importance. Category 'B' is for buildings of regional or local significance, while Category 'C' is for other buildings of architectural or historical merit. 'A' listed buildings form about 8 per cent of all the listed buildings in Scotland. In Edinburgh, the ratio is more than double that, at 19 per cent. Large parts of the Old and New Towns are listed wholesale, including many entire streets.

As well as the historic houses, churches, palaces and mansions you would expect to be so listed, there is a very wide range of other structures.

The Usher concert hall on Lothian Road and the King's Theatre on Leven Street are both 'A' listed, as are the Waterloo Hotel on Waterloo Place, the former Scotsman Hotel, and a dozen other hotels.

Twenty-one public houses, bars and taverns are 'A' listed, including Deacon Brodie's Tavern on Lawnmarket, the Café Royal on West Register Street, the Kenilworth Bar in Rose Street and the Central and Northern Bars on Leith Walk. Inspector Rebus' (and Ian Rankin's) favourite pub, the Oxford Bar on Young Street, is 'B' listed.

Perhaps less predictable is the number of industrial and commercial sites that are listed buildings. The former William Ramsay Technical Institute on Inchview Terrace, for example, built in 1906, owes its Category 'A' listing to it being one of the first reinforced concrete structures in the country. The former Carron warehouses at Leith docks, built in the 1820s, are 'A' listed because they are the oldest surviving multi-storey dock warehouses in Britain, while the 1930s Imperial Dock Grain Elevator at the docks is 'B' listed. The central bus garage on Annandale Street is 'B' listed, as is the former Shrubhill tramway workshops and power station, and the former coal-fired power generating station on McDonald Road.

Warriston Cemetery, Dean Cemetery and Greyfriars Kirkyard are all 'A' listed, and the statue of Greyfriars Bobby has the same status.

MODERN LISTED BUILDINGS

We expect buildings from previous eras to be valued; perhaps more surprising is the number of post-war structures that have been given statutory protection. In total fifty-five Edinburgh buildings erected between 1946 and the 1990s are listed. Given that post-war British architecture has often been less than pleasing on the eye, the inclusion of some of these buildings has been as controversial as their first appearance.

Edinburgh University's redevelopment of George Square, for example, which involved the demolition of several Georgian houses, was widely regarded at the time as an architectural disaster. Now the skyscraper of David Hume Tower and the Brutalist hulk of Hudson Beare lecture theatre are 'A' and 'B' listed respectively, while three other concrete university buildings on the square are also listed. The university's Swedish-style Pollock Halls of Residence on Holyrood Park Road is a more popular choice for listing.

The utilitarian HMSO Store at Sighthill Industrial Estate was 'A' listed because it is the first multi-storey building in Europe constructed in pre-stressed concrete. The listing of the telephone exchanges at Fountainbridge, Woodcroft (Pitsligo Road) and Waverley (East London Street), meanwhile, reflected their post-war role in emplacing new technology in a burgeoning city. A similar technological significance attaches to the listed five-storey laboratory tower of GEC Marconi on Crewe Road North.

Some eyebrows might be raised at the listing of two office blocks on St Andrew Square, the public shelters on West Princes Street Gardens, the British Home Stores department store and other blocky structures on Princes Street, and the stacked pentagons of Scottish Widows' vast headquarters on Dalkeith Road. Perhaps less controversial are three icons of modern Edinburgh – the Forth Road Bridge, the Royal Commonwealth Pool, and the angular Expressionist-style Mortonhall Crematorium.

Other buildings are included for their social significance. The Thistle Foundation Estate on and around Niddrie Mains Road was established in 1946 specifically for disabled ex-servicemen and their families, making it one of the first disabled-adapted sets of social housing in the country. A listed group of houses on Salveson Crescent, meanwhile, was originally built for the needs of lighthouse keepers and their families.

Many people would perhaps not recognise the modernist Old Kirk of Edinburgh on Pennywell Road and Craigsbank Parish Church as churches at all, contrasting with the 'A' listed Robin Chapel on Niddrie Mains Road, dating from 1949, which seems to harmoniously join the Middle Ages to the twentieth century.

Adam House on Chambers Street looks like an eighteenth-century neo-classical building – but it was erected in 1954. In the same year the crowstepped Nisbet of Dirleton's House at 82-84 Canongate was cleverly rebuilt using some stones from the seventeenth-century original. Both are 'B' listed. Other Canongate redevelopments, at numbers 191-193, 242-244 and 249-263, again bring a subtle modern take on the tradition of Scottish vernacular urban tenement architecture – in fact, much of Canongate, which looks ancient, actually owes its appearance to the 1950s.

Other modern 'can-you-tell-the-difference?' replicas of historic buildings can be found at 98-102 West Bow, 2-3 Queen Street, 40 and 42 George Street, 114-116 George Street, and Fishmarket Square and Main Street in Newhaven. Another development of tenements and town houses in Newhaven (Great Michael Rise, Annfield and New Lane) imitates the patterns and colours of historic fishing towns

The listings also include a number of private commissions for one-off houses in Modernist styles, with striking examples in Cramond, Nether Liberton, Ravelston Dykes Road, Charterhall Road, South Queensferry and Greenhill Park.

Perhaps the most unusual 'A' listed modern structure is a greenhouse. The 420ft-long greenhouse at the Royal Botanic Garden, built in 1967, pushes its supporting structure *outside* the glass, thus maximising the available light and allowing tall trees to flourish in an uninterrupted open space. The official booklet on the post-war listed buildings of Edinburgh states that the building of the greenhouse was, 'the most important event in the annals of glasshouse construction since the nineteenth century… construction of the Kew Palm House.'

EDINBURGH'S UGLIEST BUILDING?

Most people would probably vote the St James Centre on Leith Street as the city's least-loved building. Completely out of place in the World Heritage architectural context of the New Town, the grim 1970s concrete shopping centre was supposed to have been replaced by 2015, but the project has suffered delays.

CHURCHES

St Giles Church, one of the centrepieces of the Royal Mile, has had more facelifts than a Morningside dowager. After the Reformation it was parcelled up into several different churches, eventually housing – in one building – the High Kirk, the Old Kirk, the Tolbooth Kirk and the Little Kirk (also known as Haddo's Hole). To this were added the Police Offices. All these partitions have since been removed, and the cops no longer operate out of the north transept.

Morningside Church has the longest aisle of any parish church in the UK.

Beatrix Watson, accused of witchcraft in 1649, was locked up overnight in the tower of Corstorphine Church. The following morning the church bell was heard ringing incessantly. On unlocking the door, the church officers found that Beatrix had hanged herself with the bell rope.

An indoor labyrinth can be found marked on the floor of the University Chaplaincy Centre in Bristo Square. Walking the route in a meditative, steady manner will take about thirty minutes. A similar labyrinth is laid out in a corner of George Square Gardens nearby.

LOST MONASTERIES

As with many medieval cities, Edinburgh was once dotted with monasteries, friaries and convents. And as with most Scottish cities, these religious establishments have largely disappeared as a result of the chaos and destruction unleashed during the sixteenth-century Reformation.

One of the earliest monastic houses in Edinburgh was a Dominican (Blackfriars) Friary, founded in 1230 around what is now High School Yards south of Cowgate. Although a large, walled structure, not a trace of it exists today.

The only Dominican convent in Scotland was established in the second decade of the sixteenth century in what is now Newington. Part of it was later taken over by the Nunnery of St Catherine of Sienna. The only thing left is the name, surviving in both St Catherine's Place and Sienna Place and (in its corrupted form) Sciennes Road.

Greyfriars Kirk and Kirkyard, famous for its association with the National Covenant and Greyfriars Bobby, stands on the site of a fifteenth-century Franciscan friary, destroyed, as were so many others, during the Reformation.

A monastery of Carmelite Friars (Whitefriars) was founded at Greenside on the northwest side of Calton Hill in 1526. After it was dissolved it became a leper hospital, with an integral permanent gallows; if any patient suffering from leprosy attempted to escape, they would be hanged without trial.

Another Carmelite friary stood on Hopetoun Road in South Queensferry. Fragments of the friary church remain in the present Episcopal Church.

The fate of the Augustinian Abbey of Holyrood was different to the other religious buildings. Founded in 1128 during the reign of David I, the abbey gave its name to both Abbeyhill just to the north and the Canongate area of the Royal Mile, as the latter was the domain of the canons or monks of the abbey. One of the grandest and richest monastic establishments in Scotland, it frequently hosted parliaments and royal guests as a substitute for a palace. Instead of being lost at the Reformation, the abbey was severely damaged by an English incursion in 1543, during the War of the Rough Wooing, and then suffered a mob assault in 1688. The roof was replaced but proved to be too heavy for the walls, and in 1768 it collapsed. The roofless ruin is now a picturesque part of the Palace of Holyroodhouse; in 1829 the mossy ruins inspired Felix Mendolssohn to write his *Scottish Symphony*.

SANCTUARY!

Holyrood Abbey had the power of sanctuary, which meant that those who reached the precincts and claimed sanctuary were protected from arrest or harm. In 1337 Robert Prendergast, a Scot working for the English garrison in the castle, fell out with the Governor, Thomas Knyton, and murdered him on the High Street. Prendergast then leapt on Knyton's horse and galloped down the Royal Mile to Holyrood, where he claimed sanctuary. The English posted guards around the church, hoping to starve Prendergast out, but the monks secretly fed the fugitive by lowering down provisions on a rope when the guards were inattentive late at night. After twelve days Prendergast escaped, disguised as a monk.

After the Reformation the right of sanctuary for all crimes was removed, but the grounds of Holyrood remained a refuge for debtors, where they were safe from creditors and the less-than-gentle baillies who enforced debt recovery. At one point 6,500 debtors were living permanently around Holyrood. These 'Abbey Lairds' formed a veritable community, often building their own houses, and it was common to see them taking a stroll within the confines of Holyrood Park, part of the 5-mile circumference of the refuge. The debtors were allowed out on Sunday to attend church, and no hand could be laid upon them as long as they returned to the precincts by midnight.

In 1795 Holyrood Palace was the official home of the Comte d'Artois, who many years later in 1826 became His Most Christian Majesty King Charles X of France. The Comte, Louis XVI's younger brother, had fled the French Revolution, and stayed in diplomatic asylum in Edinburgh for four years. The choice of Holyrood was no coincidence as there he was also spared the depredations of his many creditors. Charles X returned to Holyrood in 1830, having, after just a few years as the King of France, been kicked out by his countrymen.

The debtors' refuge was abolished in 1880 when debt became no longer an imprisonable offence in law. However, the law establishing the ancient right of sanctuary has never actually been repealed, so theoretically a criminal could seek safety within the grounds of Holyrood – although I wouldn't put money on it.

POPULATION

Before the advent of reliable censuses, population estimates were pretty hit-and-miss, but it looks like about 12,000 people lived in the city in the early 1500s. This figure had doubled by 1618, and reached between 50,000 and 60,000 by 1700. At this point, 'Edinburgh' meant just the Old Town; the overcrowding around the Royal Mile must have been intense.

The city's population topped 100,000 in the early nineteenth century, perpetuating the social ills of chronic overcrowding and appalling sanitation. Infectious diseases, poor quality water, animal and human waste, uncollected rubbish, widespread vermin – all these contributed to a lower than average life expectancy and a higher than average mortality rate. The agricultural and industrial revolutions continued to promote immigration into the cities, however, and the population rocketed: 138,000 in 1820, 170,000 in 1851.

These days Edinburgh's residents have a much higher life expectancy at birth – 76.2 years for males and 81.0 years for females, 40 per cent higher than it was 200 years ago.

Social changes in the late twentieth century – such as the extension of the city's boundaries, the provision of council housing, and the general availability of the motor car – have greatly expanded the area where the inhabitants of the City of Edinburgh currently live.

In 2011 514,100 people lived in Edinburgh, 6.2 per cent more than a decade previously. The city is home to 9.7 per cent of the total Scottish population.

THE MARCH OF TIME – LOST BURGHS AND BOUNDARIES

Boundaries have always been fluid things, changing as power expands and contracts. It was not until AD 1020, for example, that Edinburgh actually became part of the nation of Scotland.

Edinburgh only became the capital of Scotland as late as 1437.

The city boundaries of Edinburgh were once largely confined to Castle Rock and the upper part of the Royal Mile. The present-day street of Canongate, the lower part of the Royal Mile, was a completely separate burgh. Like all burghs, it had its own municipal administration and laws. Canongate lost most of its independence in 1630, but it was not until 1856 that the area became entirely part of Edinburgh.

1856 also saw Edinburgh swallow up Holyrood, St Cuthbert's, Pleasance, North Leith, and Coalhill in South Leith, all of which were previously outside its boundaries.

Edinburgh had already been expanding in the Georgian period. From the later eighteenth century onwards the New Town colonised farmland to the north of the Old Town. The year 1809 saw the annexation of the village of Silvermills. In 1829 the growing New Town absorbed the burghs of Calton and Broughton and the villages of Moutrie and Picardy.

Portobello developed into an independent burgh in 1833, becoming part of Edinburgh in 1896.

The year 1920 saw the great expansion: Cramond, Davidson's Mains, Corstorphine, Juniper Green, Colinton, Fairmilehead, Liberton, Gilmerton and Craigmillar all became part of Edinburgh for the first time, as did, after great resistance, the Port of Leith, which up till then had resolutely defended its independence.

The Clermiston Estate was bought from the owners by the city in the 1950s, to build local authority housing.

Changes in local authority boundaries are so numerous as to be baffling. Edinburgh's hinterland, Lothian, is now three counties – West Lothian, Midlothian and East Lothian. Midlothian, however, was once known as Edinburghshire, while the border between Midlothian and Edinburgh has swung back and forth, and the city has also bitten chunks out of West and East Lothian.

In the later nineteenth century the Town Council of Edinburgh became Edinburgh Corporation, a single-tier authority responsible for virtually every aspect of local government. Bizarrely, Midlothian County Council, which oversaw the part of Midlothian outside the city, was actually based in the centre of Edinburgh.

Edinburgh Corporation went the way of all flesh during a local government shake-up in 1975, only to be replaced by two bodies, Lothian Regional Council and the City of Edinburgh District Council, leading to confusion over which authority was responsible for what. A new single-tier local authority, the City of Edinburgh, was re-established in 1996.

UNIVERSITIES

The city has five universities, which between them support over 60,000 students a year.

The University of Edinburgh (founded in 1583). The largest and oldest of the city's universities, with a significant base in the Old Town and environs. In 2011 it was ranked by *The Times Higher Education* as the 7th top university in Europe and the 36th top university in the world.

Heriot-Watt University (founded 1855 as Heriot-Watt College, and a university since 1966), one of the premier universities in the UK for business and industry. Heriot-Watt welcomed women through its doors in 1869, a full twenty years before other similar institutions followed suit.

The Edinburgh College of Art (founded 1906, although with antecedents dating back to the eighteenth century). The college merged with the University of Edinburgh in 2011.

Edinburgh Napier University (founded 1964 as Napier Technical College, and a university since 1992). Napier has been very much seen as a 'vocational' institution. It has four principal campuses: Sighthill, Craiglockhart, Merchiston and Craighouse.

Queen Margaret University (founded 1972 as Queen Margaret College, and, having absorbed several other institutions, a university since 2007). The university's brand-new purpose-built campus is at Musselburgh. An early predecessor of both the university and the college was the Edinburgh College of Domestic Science on Atholl Crescent, widely known as the Dough School.

SCHOOLS

Edinburgh's moneyed classes supported several high-quality fee-paying schools, but provision for those further down the scale was limited. The first Ragged School or Industrial School, an institution set up to educate poor children, was founded by clergyman Dr Guthrie in Ramsay Gardens in 1847.

Generations of readers and filmgoers will be familiar with the chaotic and criminal antics of the girls of St Trinians, created by cartoonist Ronald Searle in 1946. Searle, it seems, had a real-life model for his scandalous schoolgirls. In 1922 Miss Catherine Fraser Lee founded St Trinnean's School for Girls at 10 Palmerston Road in Newington.

Sixty pupils were educated under the Dalton system of self-reliance and individual responsibility, where discipline was sometimes imposed by the girls themselves rather than by the staff. As a result outsiders called the place the 'school of do what you like', although I seriously doubt this included St Trinian's-type antics such as gambling, hooch-distilling and bomb-making.

St Trinnean's moved to St Leonard's Hall in 1925. Now the administration offices of the Pollock Halls of Residence, the hall has a conference room named 'St Trinneans': food fights and armed insurrection are not encouraged.

The 'biography' of Ian Fleming's super-spy James Bond shows that he was expelled from an Edinburgh public school, the real-life Fettes School.

FIRES

Overcrowded Edinburgh, bursting with inflammable materials, was always a major fire risk. In 1700 several of the tallest tenements around Parliament Square on the Royal Mile burned down, and in 1824 a blaze raged through the Old Town for three days, killing thirteen people, two of whom were firefighters. A thousand people were made homeless by what became known as the Great Fire. The flames were only brought under control when wet weather interceded.

The Edinburgh Fire Establishment, the first municipal fire brigade in the whole of Britain, had been formed just a few months before the Great Fire. Although they did sterling work, their hand-hauled fire engines were too wide for some of the narrow closes where the flames had taken hold, and confusion reigned among competing authorities at the scene.

Edinburgh's Master of Fire Engines, James Braidwood, used the lessons of the Great Fire to write the definitive manual on firefighting, which for the first time created a clear chain of command during a fire emergency. Braidwood later founded the London Fire Brigade. A statue to this 'father of modern firefighting' stands in Parliament Square, close to the epicentre of the inferno of 1824.

On 7 December 2002 a blaze in a tall building on Cowgate took three days to be brought under control, another reminder of the difficulties of fighting fires in the Old Town.

EMBASSIES AND CONSULATES

There are currently no embassies in Edinburgh, or indeed anywhere in Scotland. The city does however host consulates from fifty-two countries:

Australia	Austria	Bangladesh
Belgium	Canada	Chile
China	Croatia	Cyprus
Czech Republic	Denmark	Finland
France	Germany	Ghana
Greece	Hungary	Iceland
India	Ireland	Israel
Italy	Japan	Jordan
Latvia	Luxembourg	Malawi
Malta	Monaco	Mongolia
Namibia	Netherlands	New Zealand
Norway	Pakistan	Philippines
Poland	Portugal	Romania
Russian Federation	Rwanda	Slovak Republic
Slovenia	South Africa	Spain
Sweden	Switzerland	Thailand
Tunisia	Turkey	Ukraine
USA		

There are also offices representing the European Commission and the European Parliament.

In the 1930s the Icelandic Consul was Sugusteinn Magnússon, whose son, Magnus Magnússon, attended Edinburgh Academy and grew up to be one of the best-known presenters on British television, acting as the quizmaster on *Mastermind* for twenty-five years.

EDINBURGHS OVERSEAS

Edinburghs – with various spellings, such as Edinburg, Edinboro or Edinborough – can be found all over the world. Many were established by Scots émigrés.

Australia

Part of Adelaide is known as Edinburgh. Being an industrial suburb, it has a population of only 168.

Queensland is home to Mount Edinburgh and the Edinburgh Range.

Canada

New Edinburgh, part of Canadian capital Ottawa, has a population of 3,627.

Another (much smaller) New Edinburgh can be found in Nova Scotia. The community was founded by Scots who had fought in the American Revolutionary War.

Edinburgh Island is an uninhabited island in the Kitikmeot Region, in Nunavut, the largest Canadian territory and one of the least-populated parts of the planet.

Guyana

Edinburgh is a rural spot west along the coast from Georgetown, the capitol of this tropical South American country.

Panama

New Edinburgh was name given to the main settlement of the ill-fated (not to say disastrous) Scottish attempt to colonize the Darien Peninsula in the 1690s. The village was abandoned amidst a nightmare of suffering and mismanagement.

Saint Helena, Ascension and Tristan da Cunha

Here, in this South Atlantic overseas territory of the United Kingdom, we find the gloriously-named Edinburgh of the Seven Seas, the main community on the island of Tristan da Cunha. The locals call it The Settlement or The Village. Edinburgh of the Seven Seas has a population of 264 and is 1,350 miles (2,173km) from the next nearest habitation, that being the equally remote island of Saint Helena. This makes Edinburgh of the Seven Seas not only the most remote 'Edinburgh' anywhere, but also the most remote permanent human settlement in the entire world.

Saint Vincent and the Grenadines

Edinboro is a small community on the outskirts of Kingston, the capitol of this island Caribbean nation.

South Africa

Edinburgh is a tiny community in Mpumalanga Province, northwest of the Sabi Sand Game Reserve.

Edinburg Farm, also in Mpumalanga Province, can be found not far from the Swaziland border. Another farm of the same name is in North-West Province.

A third Edinburgh Farm is near Hopetown in the Northern Cape Province. The farm is surrounded by other Scottish placenames such as Brechin, Forfar and Bannockburn.

USA

There are seventeen Edinburghs in the United States. Here they are, in order of population:

Edinburg, Texas (pop. 79,147). The city was originally named Chapin after one of the first developers, Dennis Chapin, but when, in typical Texas fashion, Chapin was involved in a murder/shoot-out, the council voted to rename their community as Edinburg.

Edinboro, Pennsylvania (pop. 6,950). Home to Edinboro University, which has more students than there are residents in the actual town.

Edinburgh, Indiana (pop. 4,480). Like many American Edinburghs, it is pronounced 'Edinburg' with a hard 'g'.

Edinburg Township, Ohio (pop. 2,586) is a spread-out community in the flat rural heartland.

Edinburg, New York (pop. 1,384). A village in the lovely Adirondack Park, in the rural northwest of New York State.

Edinburg, Illinois (pop. 1,135). This rural Midwest village is in Christian County.

Edinburg, Virginia (pop. 1,041) is in the Shenandoah Valley, part of the scenic Blue Ridge Mountains.

Edinburg, North Dakota (pop. 196). This Edinburg describes itself online as, 'The kind of small town every other small town would like to be.' It claims to have the only palm tree in North Dakota, a state notorious for its hard winters.

Edinburg, Maine (pop. 98). This tiny village was founded by Scottish pioneer John Bennoch in the early nineteenth century.

Edinburgh, Iowa (pop. 0). The Edinburgh Historical Village and Museum advertises itself as 'Edinburgh Ghost Town' and consists of eleven original and reconstructed historic buildings, including a courthouse and jail.

Many other American Edinburghs are simply 'places' in larger areas:

Edinburgh, North Carolina, is an outlier of the village of Wagram (pop. 765).
Edinburgh, South Carolina, is a community in the city of Columbia.
Edinburg, Mississippi, is a tiny rural crossroads.
Edinborough, Florida, is a site in the lake country north of Tampa.
A place called Edinburgh is in the city of Gaithersburg, Maryland.
Edinburg, New Jersey, is part of the City of Trenton.
Edinburg, Pennsylvania, is part of the urban area of New Castle.
Edinburgh Forest is on the edge of Frederick, Maryland.

Titusville, Pennsylvania (pop. 5,602) was settled in 1796 and originally called Edinburgh. And present-day Edinburg, Missouri, was once known as 'Buck Snort'.

Zimbabwe

Edinburgh Farm is south of the capital Harare. There is also a Morningside in the city of Bulawayo.

DUNEDINS AROUND THE WORLD

'Dunedin' is often used as Anglicisation of the Gaelic *Dùn Éideann* or Dun Eidyn, which some people think was an earlier name for Edinburgh. There are Dunedins throughout the former British Empire, in Western Australia, South Africa, Zimbabwe and Ontario, as well as in the USA (Florida and Virginia). The best-known and largest Dunedin is on the South Island of New Zealand, where the cool maritime climate sometimes echoes that of the Scottish original. The Kiwi Dunedin also has a Portobello nearby.

TWIN TOWNS

Edinburgh is twinned with twelve cities around the world:

Aalborg, Denmark
Dunedin, New Zealand
Florence, Italy
Kiev, Ukraine
Kraków, Poland
Kyoto, Japan
Nice, France
Munich, Germany
San Diego, USA
Santa Cruz de la Sierra, Bolivia
Vancouver, Canada
Xi'an, China

During the 1978 twinning with San Diego, Edinburgh donated a copy of the statue of Greyfriars Bobby to the Californian city. The Americans responded with a copy of their statue of Bum, a three-legged itinerant who became the San Diego 'town dog' in the 1890s. Bum can be seen in Princes Street Gardens.

PRINCES STREET GARDENS

West Princes Street Gardens stand on ground reclaimed in 1820 from the Nor' Loch, a virtual open sewer that once lay in the valley here. East Princes Street Gardens, divided from their partner by The Mound, were created a decade later. Together they form the most popular green space in Edinburgh today, although for decades the gardens were private, only open to the well-heeled keyholders from the upmarket houses on Princes Street. After a long period of attrition between the New Town proprietors and the Town Council, the gardens were thrown open to all in 1876.

The world-renowned Floral Clock in West Princes Street Gardens was first planted in 1903 and takes 30,000 dwarf plants to create a new design each year.

The gardens are home to an amazingly diverse concentration of public monuments and memorials. The most prominent, and a major player in the Edinburgh skyline, is the Scott Monument, the largest monument in the world to a writer (in this case, Sir Walter Scott). The neo-Gothic spire may remind those readers of a certain vintage of the spaceship *Thunderbird 3*.

Statues in the gardens honour the memory of people still well known today, as well as others whose reputations have faded. They include:

David Livingstone, African explorer and missionary.
John Wilson, acerbic writer for *Blackwood's Edinburgh Magazine* (under the pseudonym Christopher North).
Adam Black, founder of the A&C Black publishing company, and a former Lord Provost.
Allan Ramsay, eighteenth-century Edinburgh poet.
Thomas Guthrie, church reformer and founder of the Ragged Schools for poor children.
James Young Simpson, pioneer of obstetrics and the use of chloroform, the anaesthetic properties of which he discovered by experimenting on himself; he woke up on the floor.

The elaborate Celtic Cross commemorates Dean Ramsay, a leading Victorian churchman and author of the hugely popular *Reminiscences of Scottish Life and Character*.

Dean Ramsay wasn't impressed with the five naked female forms adorning the grandiose gold-coloured Ross Fountain, which today is an elaborate landmark within the gardens.

There are numerous war memorials in the gardens. The understated semi-circle of plinths of the regimental memorial for the Royal Scots contrasts with the bold bronze equestrian statue commemorating the Royal Scots Greys. The model for the latter was Sergeant-Major Hinnigan and his horse Polly.

The Scottish American War Memorial features a young soldier, a rifle on his knees, about to answer The Call – the name of the memorial. This moving statue is a tribute to American support for Scotland during the First World War.

The boulder of the Norwegian Brigade War Memorial is inscribed with a heartfelt thank you message to Scotland: 'During the War Years 1940-45 The Norwegian Brigade and their Army Units were raised and trained in Scotland. Here we found hospitality, friendship and hope during dark years of exile. In grateful memory of our Friends and Allies on these Isles this Stone was erected in the year 1978.'

Another stone stands to the memory of local men who fought in the International Brigade of the Spanish Civil War, 1936-39. The verse inscribed on the stone notes that the volunteers fought not for glory, money or patriotism – 'Their call was a cry of anguish from the hearts of the people of Spain.'

Appropriately for a park, many of the memorials are in the form of trees. The Workers Memorial Tree commemorates workers who died as a result of work-related illnesses and accidents. The Chinese Birch Tree memorialises those who died during the Tiananmen Square protests of 1989, while the United Nations Tree, planted in 1985, marks the 40th Anniversary of the United Nations, and the three Dawyck beeches remember garden superintendents from the 1930s and 1940s: Mr Docherty, Mr White and Mr Grant.

Robert Louis Stevenson is commemorated both in nature (a grove of silver birch trees) and stone (a simple pedestal marked 'RLS – A MAN OF LETTERS 1850-1894'). Stevenson explicitly stated he did not want a statue in his memory.

The one statue in the gardens that does not commemorate a person or group shows a woman wearing a crown attended by two children displaying plans and applying mortar to a pillar. This is a representation of an abstraction: the Genius of Architecture.

SOME COMMON
EDINBURGH URBAN MYTHS

Myth: John Knox's house on High Street was once owned by John Knox.
Reality: Not only did the Protestant firebrand not own the house, he probably never even lived there. The owner was another man by the name of Knox, hence the confusion. However, the belief that the leading figure of the Scottish Reformation had an association did fortunately lead to the preservation of this wonderful sixteenth-century building, which is now the Scottish Storytelling Centre.

Myth: The building of the New Town to the north of the Old Town was the first time Edinburgh expanded outside its walls.
Reality: An upmarket residential area to the south of the Old Town was actually built in 1766, a few months before the New Town was started. Unfortunately the South Side area, centred on George Square and Bristo Square, was redeveloped by the university after the Second World War, destroying many of the fine old houses and replacing them with concrete hideousness. So Edinburgh's first Georgian 'new town' has been forgotten.

Myth: Burke and Hare were body-snatchers.
Reality: Body-snatchers were grave robbers, digging bodies out of recent graves to sell to the anatomists. William Burke and William

Hare, whose crimes were exposed in 1828, avoided the risky business of visiting graveyards by simply killing their victims and selling the fresh corpses directly. Burke and Hare were not body-snatchers, but murderers.

2

RIVERS, LOCHS
AND CANALS

Edinburgh is unusual in that, unlike cities such as London, Glasgow and Aberdeen, it is not built on the banks of a great river. It was not access to a navigable waterway that determined the location of the city, but the defensive opportunities afforded by Castle Rock.

THE WATER OF LEITH

It is possible to visit or even live in Edinburgh and not notice its principal river. The Water of Leith is often obscured from sight by urban development and the up-down topography of the city. For those

who do discover it, however, the Water of Leith can become a source of great pleasure, a ribbon of silvery water and greenery amidst the stone and brick.

The modest river rises in the Pentland Hills and runs for 24 miles through Currie, Colinton, Saughton, Dean Village, Stockbridge and Inverleith, a route that barely touches the city centre. Indeed, it wasn't until the early nineteenth century that the river was included within the expanding city boundaries.

Although it was recorded as the *aqua de Lethe* in 1398, the Water of Leith has nothing to do with the Water of Lethe, which, in Greek mythology, ran through Hades, where it caused the spirits of the dead to forget their earthly life. 'Leith' may mean 'damp' or 'moist'.

Danube Street, built about 1825, was probably named after the mighty European river because of the street's proximity to the Water of Leith. The Danube, however, is seventy-five times longer, and its delta is larger than Edinburgh.

The river exit at Leith created a natural harbour long before the docks were built, creating a resource vital for Edinburgh's trade.

The Water of Leith and other streams flooded in April 2000, causing around £25 million of damage. The rate of water flow in the Water of Leith, Braid Burn and Gogar Burn was the highest ever recorded for those waterways. The flood was categorised by the Scottish Environment Protection Agency (SEPA) as a 1 in 180 year event.

The Industrial Revolution harnessed the river to drive waterwheels at seventy-six closely-packed mills producing everything from grain, meal and woodflour (for linoleum), to textiles, spices and snuff. Esparto grass was imported for the manufacture of paper; of the four paper mills, one specialised in producing paper for a very Edinburgh product – banknotes.

In 1874 the Balerno branch of the Caledonian Railway was built specifically to serve twenty-two mills on the Water of Leith. The last snuff mill didn't close until the Second World War, and a tannery was still operating into the 1950s.

This concentration of industry turned the river into a stinking chemical soup. The closure of all the mills, and the dedicated efforts of conservation groups, has brought the Water of Leith back to life. Fish have returned to the river, and brown trout weighing up to 1.6kg have been caught in the lower reaches, below the weirs. Orchids can be seen in some areas, kingfishers glimpsed, and otters have been spotted.

The delightful Water of Leith Walkway now stretches for more than 12 miles between Balerno and Leith, with a visitor centre at the halfway point near Slateford.

In 2010 the celebrated British artist Antony Gormley installed six life-size figures in the river between the Scottish National Gallery of Modern Art and the sea at Leith. The enigmatic sculptures attracted huge attention, and some were quickly 'pimped out' with bikinis, woolly hats and underwear.

The statues were fitted with a mechanism that allowed them to tilt if the pressure of water became too much. This mechanism failed on four statues, causing them to be temporarily removed.

In Paul Johnston's 1999 novel *Water of Death*, the Water of Leith becomes the site for a series of gruesome murders.

OTHER EDINBURGH RIVERS

The River Almond rises in the Pentland Hills and decants into the Forth at Cramond on the west side of Edinburgh. Migratory brown trout can be found in its waters. It is hard to imagine now, but the stretch between Cramond Brig and the sea was once a small cluster of heavy industry, with five iron mills, driven by water-wheels, churning out large quantities of nails and other small metal products.

A small passenger ferry used to cross the river at Cramond. The passenger fee in 1947 was 2*d*. In 2001, the year the ferry ran for the last time, it was 50p. The penultimate ferryman was Rudolph 'Val' Badura, a Czech who escaped from the Nazis. He operated the single-oared ferry for thirty-eight years from 1951 to 1989, and, for relaxation, swam around Cramond Island almost every day during that time.

On the east side of the city, the River Esk skirts round the south of Edinburgh for just over 4 miles, to emerge into the sea at Musselburgh, while the Braid Burn/Figgate Burn meanders through Duddingston onto its exit at Portobello, and the Brunstane Burn/Niddrie Burn heads from Brunstane to the Forth at Joppa.

As well as crossing roads and railways, the Union Canal uses aqueducts to cross the River Almond, the Gogar Burn, the Murray Burn and the Water of Leith. The last is crossed at Slateford by a spectacular water-over-water eight-arched aqueduct 500ft long and 75ft high.

THE FIRTH OF FORTH

It is arguable whether the Forth is in any way still a river at Edinburgh, as the water is salty as far upstream as the Kincardine Bridge further west. The great estuary is known as the Firth of Forth, 'firth' coming from the same root as the Norwegian word 'fjord'.

The Firth of Forth provides Edinburgh, via Leith, with access to the North Sea and Europe. It is the only sheltered anchorage on Britain's east coast between Invergordon in Easter Ross (northern Scotland) and the Humber (eastern England) and so has been important for trade and warfare since at least the Dark Ages.

ISLANDS IN THE FORTH

The inner Firth of Forth around Edinburgh has five principal islands, all but one of them uninhabited, and all but two privately owned and out of bounds.

Inchkeith (the addition of the word 'island' is unnecessary, as 'inch' means 'island') is clearly visible from Edinburgh, being 5 miles from Leith. The long island is dominated by a now-automatic nineteenth-century lighthouse, and was once a farm, but its topography also bears extensive witness to several centuries of military use, from roads and subterranean magazines built during the Victorian era to gun batteries and searchlight emplacements from the First and Second World Wars. In the sixteenth century alone, the island was garrisoned by the English, the Italians (acting as mercenaries for the English), the French and the Scots.

In 1497 Inchkeith was used as a quarantine outpost for the first time, the patients being Edinburgh residents suffering from 'grandgore' (syphilis). In 1580 the crew of a plague-stricken ship were confined on the island, with a repeat performance in 1609. Finally, in 1799 a number of Russian sailors who had died from a fearsomely infectious disease were buried on Inchkeith.

In 1773 Dr Johnson, accompanied by his Edinburgh amanuensis James Boswell, visited the island, and declared: 'I'd have this island: I'd build a house… A rich man of a hospitable turn here, would have many visitors from Edinburgh.' Johnson may have been influenced by Inchkeith's rainfall, the lowest annual average in Scotland (21.75in).

In 1490 King James IV, an unusually inquisitive and learned monarch for the times, desired to discover the original language spoken by the earliest humans (by which he meant Adam and Eve). To remove the influences of contemporary culture and language, James isolated two infants on Inchkeith with a mute woman. A brief account of the experiment appears in *The Historie and Chronicles of Scotland, 1436–1565*, written by Robert Lindsay of Pitscottie in the sixteenth century; no details are provided, other than some people thought the children, when they reached the age of speech, spoke Hebrew. Lindsay is now widely regarded as an unreliable historian, so we cannot even be certain if this bizarre piece of linguistic research ever really did take place.

Inchmickery is a 200yd-long island about 5 miles east of Inchkeith and 2 miles north of Silverknowes in Edinburgh. Most of the land area is taken up with the remains of gun batteries from the two world wars. It is often stated that the island's ship-like silhouette was enhanced during the First World War with dummy funnels and masts, to mimic a warship and make it a false target. This oft-repeated story of 'Battleship Island' may or may not be true.

North of Inchmickery are several rocky shipping hazards, one of them identified by a light. Then comes *Inchcolm*, the only island that can be visited and the only one with a semi-permanent population (two). Both residents work for Historic Scotland. The Augustinian abbey they look after was established in the twelfth century and abandoned some 400 years later. The complex, although partly ruined, forms the best-preserved monastic buildings in Scotland, and the abbey made Inchcolm so famous it was mentioned in Shakespeare's play *Macbeth*.

Inchcolm was regarded as holy long before the abbey was built. About 1040, after defeat at the Battle of Kinghorn in Fife, the Vikings paid Danegeld to bury their slain warriors on the island. An even earlier Norse hogbacked gravestone lies on the island, and an early Christian hermit once lived here.

In the Middle Ages and later, Inchcolm suffered similar military incursions to the other Forth islands. These days, evidence is still plentiful of the fortifications built during the two world wars.

Regular ferries ply to Inchcolm from South Queensferry, the season being April to October.

Cramond Island is a tidal island reached by a mile-long causeway that is covered twice a day by the waters of the Firth (and which can leave unwary visitors stranded on the island). The causeway is guarded by impressive concrete 'teeth' erected as an anti-raider obstacle during the Second World War. Other remains of the island's wartime fortifications are easily visible.

Inchgarvie has been a fort, a state prison, a Royalist garrison (in the Civil Wars), a gun battery (in the Napoleonic Wars), a naval battery (in the First World War) and an anti-aircraft battery (in the Second World War). The remains of the defences can be clearly studied while crossing the Forth Rail Bridge, as the island forms the support for one of the cantilevers (sit on the east side of the train).

During the inter-war years many former German naval vessels were broken up at Rosyth. Much of the recycled scrap metal was sold to Germany – where it was used to build Hitler's new generation of warships. In 1928 the heavily-armoured German battlecruiser

Moltke was brought to Rosyth dockyard for scrapping. Raised from the sea bed at Scapa Flow in Orkney, the ship was actually towed upside-down, its awkward dead-weight requiring three of the most powerful ocean-going tugs in the world to pull it. When the bizarre upturned vessel entered the Forth, an argument broke out between two of the local tugs about who would perform the final tow. As the skippers shouted at each other, no one noticed that the tide had caught the *Moltke* and was pulling it towards the Forth Bridge.

The tow rope from the main tugs caught on the east point of Inchgarvie island, and, as it would have dragged the boats under, the cable was cut. This left 22,979 tons of upside-down German battlecruiser drifting out of control towards the Forth Bridge. Fortunately the massive hunk of steel and iron did not hit any of the cantilever piers, and, having safely sailed under the bridge, the vessel was captured again by the relieved tugs and guided to Rosyth.

There was another capital ship adrift in the Forth in 2001. The aircraft carrier HMS *Ark Royal*, undergoing sea trials after a refit at Rosyth, lost its rudder control. The Admiralty expressly stated that neither the road bridge nor the rail bridge had been in danger of a collision.

EDINBURGH'S SHIPS

Six Royal Navy ships have been named HMS *Edinburgh*:

1. A 32-gun warship, originally called the *Royal William* and transferred from the Royal Scottish Navy at the Act of Union in 1707. Somewhat ignominiously, she was deliberately sunk to act as a mere breakwater.
2. A 70-gun warship, originally the seventeenth-century HMS *Warspite* but renamed HMS *Edinburgh* in 1721. Having been rebuilt twice, and seen significant battle action, she was broken up in 1771, by which point she was well over 100 years old.
3. A 74-gun warship in service from 1811 to 1865, serving in campaigns in Egypt and Russia.
4. A steel-plated battleship in service from 1882 to 1910.

5. A 10,000-ton light cruiser launched in 1939, and one of the ships attacked in the Firth of Forth during the first air-raid on mainland Britain. Having performed convoy duty to Malta, West Africa and Russia, and served on campaigns in Norway and the North Atlantic, she suffered torpedo damage from a U-boat on 30 April 1942. Two days later she was fatally attacked by German destroyers in the Barents Sea, with the loss of fifty-seven men. As she was carrying £5 million in gold bullion (war payment from the USSR), the ship was deliberately scuttled to avoid the gold falling into enemy hands. The treasure, now valued at £45 million, was salvaged in 1981.

6. A Type 42 destroyer launched in 1983. 2013 marked the retirement of this much-respected workhorse ship, known as the 'Fortress of the Sea'. On a 2012 exercise she fired the last Sea Dart missile, the final deployment of the Royal Navy's anti-aircraft shield that had been in use for forty years, proving its worth in the Falklands War and the first Gulf War.

LOST LOCHS

We tend not to think of Edinburgh as a land of lochs, but there was once a great deal more surface water around in the city than there is today.

A 3-mile line of lochs and marshes once stretched from Gogar near the airport through Corstorphine to Haymarket, and this severely impeded military operations when Cromwell was fighting General Leslie's Covenanting army in 1650. Gogar Loch ran between North and South Gyle, the placename 'gyle' being derived from the Gaelic word for water. A neighbouring field was known as The Flashes ('the marshes').

Gogar Loch disappeared in 1766, while its larger neighbour, Corstorphine Loch, was first drained in 1670, but the final reclamation did not take place until as late as 1837. The principal drainage channel was a deep ditch known as The Stank. Corstorphine Castle, now lost, stood on the only dry land between the lochs of Gogar and Corstorphine, thus guarding a key access route.

The Burgh Loch, drained in the eighteenth century, lay to the south of the city. Its site is now partly occupied by the delightful green space of The Meadows.

A small loch, the King's Mire, once lay at the foot of Arthur's Seat. It was drained in the early sixteenth century to provide a garden for Holyrood Palace. The two bodies of water currently within Holyrood Park, St Margaret's Loch and Dunsapie Loch, are both artificial. The former was created in 1856 as part of the landscaping improvements by Queen Victoria's husband Prince Albert.

In 1564 Mary, Queen of Scots had a dam built across the marshy Hunter's Bog in Holyrood Park. The resulting small loch was used for a re-enactment of a naval battle from the Siege of Leith a few years' previously, the entire entertainment being put on to celebrate the wedding of two of Mary's courtiers. The fragments of the dam remain, although the loch has vanished back into the bog.

Duddingston Loch is still with us, although it once occupied more of its basin, before the drainage operations in the seventeenth and eighteenth centuries. Duddingston is a wildlife reserve, and also has a fascinating archaeology. The 'Duddingston Hoard' of fifty-three metalwork weapons and tools was dredged out of the loch in 1778, and this Bronze Age 'sacrifice' to the gods of the waters can be viewed in the National Museum of Scotland. In the early 1800s the loch also revealed the wooden remains of a crannog (an artificial island, now long gone).

The Revd Robert Walker, a member of the Edinburgh Skating Club, was immortalised skating on Duddingston Loch by Edinburgh portrait painter Sir Henry Raeburn. This famous painting, commonly called *The Skating Minister*, can be admired in the National Gallery of Scotland on The Mound. A less well known but equally serene and atmospheric painting, *Skaters on Duddingston Loch by Moonlight* by Charles Lees, is on display in a London gallery.

Lochend Loch, which used to supply the drinking water for Leith, is still in evidence off Lochend Road. Also once known as Restalrig Loch, it was here in 1576 that Bessie Dunlop, guided by her usual companion – the ghost of a dead soldier – encountered an energetic group of invisible fairies. Having confessed to these experiences, Bessie was strangled and burned for witchcraft.

The most celebrated lost loch was the Nor' Loch, which once stretched from directly below the side of the castle as far east as the present North Bridge. There are three theories about the origin of the loch: it may have been entirely natural, part of the chain of lochs running in from the west; it may have been created as a defensive measure in the 1450s, as a kind of moat; or it may have been accidentally dammed by the landslide of rubbish and human waste descending down the slope from the Old Town.

As well as being an open sewer, the Nor' Loch was often used as a place of punishment via a ducking stool, or to 'float' witches to determine their guilt, or as a site of execution for female criminals (who were sometimes drowned rather than hanged).

The Nor' Loch was progressively drained over many decades, finally disappearing in 1820, providing the land for the present-day railway line and Princes Street Gardens.

The original plan for the New Town included an ornamental stretch of water to replace the drained Nor' Loch. This particular piece of landscaping was never carried through; if it had, the users of Princes Street Gardens would today have been able to enjoy a stroll alongside something similar to the Serpentine in London's Hyde Park.

EDINBURGH'S WATER SUPPLY

With relatively few wells, Edinburgh initially had to largely rely on the Nor' Loch, which could hardly be regarded as a source of clean water.

In the 1670s the first piped water arrived in the Old Town, brought from natural springs at Comiston to the south. Each springhead was marked with a carved lead image – a swan, hare, fox and peewit (lapwing), which were probably the local names of the original springs. There may have been another carving of an owl, now lost. The four life-size figures are in the Museum of Edinburgh on Canongate, and today the area around Comiston Spring Avenue has street names such as Swan Spring Avenue and Fox Spring Rise.

The first lead pipe, 3 miles long and 3in in diameter, was installed by a German plumber resident in Newcastle. We are not told what his call-out fee was, but the pipe costs cost £2,950 to lay (about £250,000 in today's terms).

From the first moment the miraculously fresh and clean water arrived in pipes in the city centre, it was never enough for the burgeoning population. Over the centuries many more pipes were laid, reservoirs built and cisterns constructed, although the battle between water demand and water supply continued to occupy the letter columns of *The Scotsman* up until the late Victorian period and beyond.

Despite the provision of piped water elsewhere, many nineteenth-century apartments in Old Town tenements still relied on 'water carriers' to lug heavy barrels of water up the narrow stairways.

Much is made in the tourist literature of Edinburgh's 'Underground City' but there are subterranean secrets that appear on no tour guide's itinerary. A disused aqueduct tunnel, long forgotten, still runs under the city centre. The Crawley Aqueduct passes through a tunnel 2,160ft long, from the Meadows, beneath the former Royal Infirmary and the Grassmarket, and up the slope of Castle Wynd, to then cut through Castle Rock via another tunnel coming to a distribution terminus at the foot of the Mound. An inconspicuous manhole cover at the junction of the Mound and Princes Street marks the end of the tunnel, which is tall enough to walk through.

TAKING THE WATERS

A set of low stones in Corstorphine's Dunsmuir Court covers the Physic Well, to which the sick and diseased would once travel for many miles in hope that the reputed healing waters would heal them.

Once known as the 'Well of our Lady' (a reference to the Virgin Mary), this was a holy well before the Reformation swept away such examples of what was called 'Catholic superstition'. Many of the streets nearby are named 'Ladywell'.

The eighteenth century saw the height of the fashionable fad of 'taking the waters' at spas and mineral springs. The Physic Well became more commercially developed after 1745, with regular stagecoaches from Edinburgh bringing people to stay at purpose-built accommodation. By the 1790s the well was no longer in favour, perhaps because it had been eclipsed by the better-known St Bernard's Well on the banks of the Water of Leith in Stockbridge. Active as a draw for the well-to-do since 1760, in 1789 the well was aggrandised by the construction of a circular domed Classical temple complete with a marble statue of Hygeia, the Greek goddess of health and hygiene.

The wonderful temple at St Bernard's Well can be viewed externally at any time, but both it and the ornate pump room beneath can only be visited once a year on Doors Open Day in September.

The temple was commissioned by Lord Gardenstone, amongst whose many eccentricities was his fondness for pigs. On his estate in Kincardineshire (now Aberdeenshire) he allowed his pet pig to share his bed.

CANALS

Canals were the motorways of their day. The Forth and Clyde Canal, constructed in 1790, joined the River Clyde at Glasgow with the River Forth at Grangemouth. The remaining miles to Edinburgh, however, had to be completed by land. After almost three decades of proposals, counter-proposals, financial setbacks and political wrangling, a canal link all the way to Edinburgh was finally begun in 1818.

The Edinburgh and Glasgow Union Canal opened in January 1822, having cost more than two and a half times its original price estimate.

Most of the labour force were Irishmen, nicknamed 'navvies' from the word 'navigation', the original word for canal. Amongst their number were William Burke and William Hare, who later went on to infamy as the multiple murderers of the 1828 bodysnatching scandal.

The 31.5 mile-long Edinburgh and Glasgow Union Canal ran from the Port Hopetoun basin between Semple Street and Lothian Road, to Lock 16 on the Forth and Clyde Canal at Camelon. Passengers to Glasgow changed at Falkirk. Overnight 'sleeper services' were popular, although they took several hours longer than the daytime journey.

By 1836 the canal was carrying 200,000 passengers a year between Edinburgh and Glasgow, while day-long pleasure trips were run to the scenic sights of Slateford, Ratho and the Almond Aqueduct.

The coming of the railways spelled the end of the canals. The Edinburgh and Glasgow Union Canal was one of the last of its kind. The operators slashed their prices, but by the mid-1840s passenger services were withdrawn.

Goods transport continued for some time, as the canal had been designed to serve Edinburgh's need for coal, building stones, timber, sand, lime, slate, brick and meal. Port Hamilton was constructed near Port Hopetoun specifically to cope with the coal imports.

All goods landed in Edinburgh were subject to a tax of one penny per ton – except manure.

A typical canal barge or scow carried 40 tons and was pulled by one horse. Larger vessels, called lighters, required two horses. Steam scows, although available, were not used because the bridges on the Union Canal were too low for the steam funnels. A Victorian scow was dug up from the canal bank in 2004.

In 1921 Ports Hopetoun and Hamilton were abandoned and the canal shortened, so that it now terminated at Lochrin Basin in Tollcross, on the south side of Fountainbridge. The canal was officially closed to navigation in 1965 but in reality commercial traffic had ceased by the 1930s.

In 1979 the Edinburgh and Glasgow Union Canal became a Scheduled Ancient Monument.

In 2000 the Millennium Link near Falkirk reconnected the Edinburgh and Glasgow Union Canal with the Forth and Clyde Canal. The three spectacular aqueducts (over the rivers Avon and Almond, and the Water of Leith) were restored. A new stretch of canal was dug at Wester Hailes, where the original canal had been filled in. In 2002 the restored canal was officially reopened.

Edinburgh Quay, the new name for the current terminal, is an upmarket regeneration area at Fountainbridge. The canal is now used by canoeists, rowers and raft racers. Pleasure boat trips have returned. Social enterprises such as Re-Union Canal Boats engage in community projects. Walkways have been established and the canal environment is a recognised corridor for wildlife.

A number of people – known as liveaboards – reside on narrowboats in the Ratho and Lochrin basins.

From a neglected, largely forgotten repository for shopping trolleys and rubbish, the canal has become a key element of modern Edinburgh.

In the 1880s Germany opened the Kiel Canal, a massive engineering project that linked the port of Kiel on the Baltic Sea with the River Elbe. This gave the German Navy a shortcut to the North Sea, providing a strategic advantage to a nation that was starting to rival Britain's supremacy at sea. Immediately plans were scouted for a 'battleship canal' between the Firth of Forth and the Firth of Clyde, which would give the Royal Navy an equally important shortcut between the North Sea and the Atlantic. Various routes were set out for the Scottish Ship Canal (also known as the Scottish Naval Canal), with proposals put forward in 1889, 1890, 1906 and 1912, but in the end the idea was defeated by the huge cost, and Scotland's battleship canal was never built.

3

TRANSPORTS OF DELIGHT – TRAINS, TRAMS, FERRIES AND FLIGHT

ROAD TRANSPORT
BEFORE THE MOTOR CAR

The first stagecoach service in Scotland ran between Edinburgh and Leith in 1610. It failed. The service was revived fifty years later, only to fail again.

In 1678 Edinburgh merchant William Hume inaugurated a weekly stagecoach to Glasgow. The passengers – six to a coach – were each charged the high sum of four Scots pounds and sixteen shillings, and in winter this fare increased by 20 per cent. Although Mr Hume was granted all kinds of privileges, from an exclusive licence for seven years, a public subsidy from Glasgow, and an assurance that his horses would not be 'pressed' for the Army, the service failed because of the appalling quality of the roads.

In 1688 a visitor to Scotland noted that the country had no stagecoach services, and only two routes where post was carried by horse – from Edinburgh to Berwick, and from Edinburgh to Portpatrick and the boats to Ireland.

The viability of the horse-post to Portpatrick was threatened by foot couriers carrying unofficial letters along the same route. Fearing that such letters might be seditious or treasonous, the Scottish Parliament declared that the foot-post to Ireland was illegal. Elsewhere, the fastest way to send a letter from Edinburgh (to, say, Perth) was still via a man walking at 3mph.

In 1712 travellers were advised in newspaper advertisements: 'All that desire to pass from Edinbro' to London, let them repair to Mr John Baillie's at the Coach and Horses at the head of the Canongate, every other Saturday.' The operators boasted the coach could accomplish the journey in thirteen days, 'without any stoppage (if God permit).' Eighty horses were posted along the route to ensure speedy changeovers. The fare one-way was £4 10s, and each paying passenger was allowed 20lb of luggage free of charge.

In 1780 the fastest Edinburgh-London coach was making the journey in four days, reduced to forty-one hours by 1830.

On 15 April 1832 a very special coach arrived in Edinburgh, having broken all records in coming from London in thirty-six hours. Bedecked with white ribbons and rosettes, it brought the news that the House of Lords had finally passed the Reform Act, the much-fought-over legislation that saw the beginning of the end of the domination of Parliament by the landed upper classes.

By 1749 the 'Edinburgh and Glasgow Caravan', a covered spring-cart, was up and running, making the journey between the two cities in two days of boneshaking discomfort. From then on, commercial competition, road-making and improved coachbuilding technology saw a gradual improvement in services. By 1758 the daily *Edinburgh Fly* was getting to Glasgow in just twelve hours.

Intercity travel eventually reduced to eight hours, and then six, but by the time the stagecoaches had reached the astonishing heights of Edinburgh to Glasgow in just four and a half hours, the Edinburgh and Glasgow Railway opened and horse-drawn coaches dwindled into oblivion.

In the 1780s James McLehose, a law agent from Glasgow, courted Agnes Craig, despite the fact that her father had banned the young man from his daughter's presence. Mr McLehose therefore arranged to take the same stagecoach to Edinburgh as Agnes – and purchased all the other seats, ensuring he and his sweetheart could be alone. At the age of seventeen, Agnes Craig duly became Mrs James McLehose. Sadly for this tale of romance and ardour, Mr McLehose proved to be a poor husband, and after four years his persistent cruelty prompted his wife to leave him.

THE ROADS TODAY

134 people suffered death or serious injury in traffic accidents in 2010. This compares with 268 for 2001, or a 50 per cent reduction. The 2010 death toll was the lowest rate for a decade.

In 2010, 42 per cent of journeys to work by Edinburgh residents were by car. 29 per cent took the bus, 19 per cent walked and 9 per cent cycled to work. Only 2 per cent used the train – a reflection of the very limited suburban rail service in the city. Of those who commuted in from outside of the city, coming from Fife, Stirling, Falkirk and the Lothians, a higher percentage travelled by train, but the car was still king, despite clogged roads and the bottleneck at the Forth Road Bridge.

The North Edinburgh Cycle Network is the only urban cycle route in Britain that crosses a city without encountering any motor traffic.

EARLY RAILWAYS

The first railway in Edinburgh opened in July 1831, two months before its equivalent in Glasgow. Like many early railways, it did not carry passengers. The Edinburgh and Dalkeith Railway (EDR) ran south from St Leonards Depot, beside Salisbury Crags, its horse-drawn wagons being entirely devoted to transporting coal from the Lothian coalfields. One part was too steep for horsepower, so stationary steam engines were used to haul the wagons up the gradient.

The EDR's spur to Dalkeith opened in 1839, prompting the Duke of Buccleuch to build a horse-drawn tramway from the railway terminus to his coalfields east of the town.

The EDR later expanded east to Niddrie, Eskbank, Portobello and Fisherrow near Musselburgh, and north to Leith, by which point passengers were being carried in open carriages – although the crowding, confusion and to-ing and fro-ing in the third-class carriages meant that it was often too difficult to collect fares.

Byelaws forbade the train drivers from grazing horses while pulling trains.

After fourteen years the EDR was bought at a bargain price by the North British Railway, which paid less than the lines had cost to construct.

The St Leonards line is now a walkway and cycle path leading into Holyrood Park. A sign indicates the 'Innocent Railway', the sobriquet referring to the EDR's preference for horses over steam-powered locomotives.

The Edinburgh and Glasgow Railway arrived in 1842, although it terminus was just west of the city centre. The first railway reached what is now Waverley Station in 1846. Furious landowners and influential New Town residents ensured both station and line kept a low profile, which is why the massive bulk of Waverley, far from commanding its environment like other major railway stations, is hidden in a dip.

From the 1840s onward, as 'railway fever' swept the nation, several rival railway companies opened a bewildering number of routes and stations around Edinburgh, many of which later closed, merged, were relocated or renamed. As a result of this intense example of capitalism in the raw, Waverley was at one point actually three separate stations. The North British Railway and the Edinburgh and Glasgow Railway had rival stations back-to-back near North Bridge. Meanwhile, the Edinburgh, Leith and Granton Railway ran north out of Canal Street Station, which was at right angles to the first two. Each company had its own ticket office, entrance and ticketing system, which meant making a connection was fraught with difficulties – it seems frustrations over trains have always been with us!

By the time Waverley opened as a unified station in 1868, it was, in terms of platform area, the second largest station in Britain. Only London Waterloo was bigger. Waverley now sees over 19 million passenger arrivals and departures each year.

The first trains between Edinburgh and Glasgow took two and a quarter hours (compared to eight hours by canal). Currently, the journey takes between forty-five minutes and one hour.

RAILWAY TUNNELS

Edinburgh's hilly topography meant that railway tunnels were a necessity from the beginning. The Edinburgh and Dalkeith Railway had one of the earliest railway tunnels in Scotland, drilled through a rocky spur of Salisbury Crags. Today, a mainline tunnel 130 yards long burrows under The Mound west of Waverley, and then, after a brief spurt of daylight, the 1,040-yard Haymarket Tunnel disappears under Lothian Road to emerge into Haymarket Station.

The great lost tunnel of Edinburgh's railways is the Scotland Street Tunnel. Built in 1847, it runs north for 1,052 yards from Canal Street Station (the former north part of current-day Waverley), emerging at Scotland Street. The trains then continued to Granton, Newhaven and Leith, on lines that are now lost. It is unlikely that the New Town residents of St Andrews Street, Dublin Street and Drummond Place know that a grand piece of once-gaslit Victorian engineering lies below their cellars. The southern part of the tunnel was destroyed during the construction of Princes Mall shopping centre.

The Scotland Street Tunnel was closed in 1868, but has had a varied life since. Having first been used as a siding for rolling stock, it then became a mushroom farm. During the Second World War the tunnel was pressed into service as a bomb-proof telephone command and control centre for the London and North-East Railway. Some of the brick-built structures from this time still survive (it should be noted that the tunnel is unsafe and sealed off). Finally, the Physics Department of Edinburgh University briefly used the site as a laboratory, before the tunnel became a parking lot for Cochrane's Garage – although, given the gradient of the tunnel, the vehicles must have been parked with their handbrakes on.

RAILWAY RIVALRY

After various amalgamations and takeovers, two leading companies emerged. The North British Railway and the Caledonian Railway went head-to-head for many years, fighting each other tooth and nail for routes and customers. Dirty deeds were commonplace.

For example, the NBR opened the massive Leith Central Station in 1903 largely to block a planned Caledonian route from Leith to Princes Street.

In 1902 the NBR, operating out of Waverley, built the grand North British Hotel at the eastern end of Princes Street as an outward manifestation of their prestige. The CR, not to be outdone, erected the equally impressive Caledonian Hotel next to their Lothian Road terminus at the western end of Princes Street. The latter hotel's telegraphic address was 'Luxury, Edinburgh'.

In 1923, during a national railway reorganisation, the NBR was absorbed into the London and North East Railway while the Caledonian Railway became part of the London Midlands and Southern Railway. The North British Hotel is now the Balmoral, and the Caledonian Hotel is the Caledonian Hilton. The latter no longer has its terminus, Princes Street Station (known to everyone as Caley Station) having closed in 1965. The line of the track between Princes Street and Dalry Road stations is now the Western Approach Road.

In 1928 there were more than thirty passenger stations in the Edinburgh area. Currently there are eleven – Waverley, Haymarket, Slateford, Kingsknowe, Wester Hailes, Curriehill, Edinburgh Park, South Gyle, Brunstane, Newcraighall and Musselburgh.

The former station at Trinity, on the coast, had two booking windows. One was for the general public while the second was reserved for the fisherwomen, whose fishscale-covered hands gave the woodwork (and everything else) an unshiftable patina of fish grease.

In 1986 a new station was opened next to Meadowbank Stadium specifically for shuttle trains bringing passengers from Waverley to the Commonwealth Games. Always intended as a temporary structure, the station has since been removed.

The air around St Margarets Locomotive Shed was so polluted that residents in nearby Restalrig Road South could not open their windows without getting a lungful of coal smoke.

In 1937 a fire killed hundreds of pigeons nesting in the vast glass canopy of Leith Central, littering the platforms and rails with smoke-asphyxiated birds.

TRAMS

The first Edinburgh tram, drawn along guide rails by horses, set off on 6 November 1871. It ran from Haymarket Station via Princes Street and Leith Walk to Bernard Street in Leith.

Cable-hauled trams commenced on one route in 1888, but some trams in Leith were still being pulled by horses as late as 1904. The following year Leith saw the introduction of the first electric trams in Scotland. The last horse-car was put out to pasture as late as 24 August 1907, the route being from Tollcross to Colinton Road via Gilmore Place. Some of the last horse-cars were rebuilt as cable-cars and then as electrically-driven trams.

As with the train system, the early years of the tramways had a bewildering range of companies, owners and names. In 1919-20 all the trams in Edinburgh and Leith became owned by Edinburgh Corporation. Tram No.172, decorated, illuminated and painted with the legend '1871 - The Last Week - 1956', toured the entire tram system in the seven days before the final closure on 16 November 1956.

Only one original Edinburgh tramcar remains. Tram No.35, dating from 1948, can be found in the National Tramway Museum in Derbyshire.

A new tram system was proposed in the early 2000s. Construction commenced in 2008, creating traffic chaos in the city centre. After endless political, legal, technical and financial problems, the total cost of the new scheme is in excess of £1 billion, over twice that of the original estimate.

CROSSING THE FORTH – BY FERRY

The vast estuary of the Firth of Forth is Edinburgh's biggest geographical asset – and its greatest obstacle. Ferries have been operating from different parts of the Lothian coast to their opposite ports in Fife since at least the twelfth century. The crossing could take anything from sixty minutes to six hours, and was frequently hazardous. In 1123, for example, King Alexander I was shipwrecked off the island of Inchcolm, halfway across, while in 1633, thirty-three members of the royal household of King Charles I were drowned in a storm.

The principal routes were, from the west: South Queensferry to North Queensferry; Granton, Newhaven or Leith to Burntisland or Pettycur (Kingshorn) in Fife; and, to the far east, North Berwick to Earlsferry near Elie.

In 1475, the Leith-Kingshorn ferry was charging two pennies for a passenger and sixpence for a horse, while fares on the much shorter Queensferry route were a penny and two pennies respectively.

In the eighteenth century the first turnpike (toll) road in Scotland linked Edinburgh with South Queensferry. The route became Scotland's most used ferry, but poor embarking/disembarking facilities, combined with erratic service, prompted endless complaints. The ferrymen all lived in North Queensferry and so usually 'parked' there, meaning passengers at the southern terminus had to wait for many hours, or even overnight. By 1809 the ferries were better regulated and kept to a timetable. In 1821 sails and oars were replaced by the first steam-driven ferry, which cut the Queensferry transit to twenty minutes.

The introduction of first steam ferries and then railways saw competing ports fighting for custom, the determining factor being railway/ship transfer facilities. In 1848, for example, the railway came to Burntisland in Fife, meaning the ferries from Granton now landed there instead of at Pettycur a few miles further east. Pettycur Harbour, the main port since 1760, immediately went into steep economic decline.

1851 saw a major innovation – the floating railway. Loaded goods wagons arriving at Granton were shunted directly from the railway terminus onto the rails aboard a flat steam ferry, sailed across 5 miles of water, and pulled off in the same way at Burntisland to be coupled to a new locomotive for the next part of the journey north. This was the first roll-on/roll-off train ferry in the world. Passengers, meanwhile, went by paddle-steamer.

The opening of the Forth Rail Bridge in 1890 eliminated the need for the railway ferry, and had a severe impact on the Queensferry ferries operating in the bridge's shadow. However, as there was still no vehicular bridge, it was the rise of the motor car that saved the Queensferry route. By the First World War the ferries were busier than they had ever been, partly through the number of vehicles servicing the new naval base at Rosyth on the Fife side.

In 1955 more than 2 million passengers and 90,000 vehicles were using the Queensferry Passage Ferry. As well as cars, lorries and pedestrians, the ferries took all forms of livestock – the minimum fare for a small car was 3s 6d, while a bull was charged at 4s. Passengers were 5d, the same fare as a sheep or goat.

The Queensferry ferries were finally withdrawn when the Forth Road Bridge was opened in 1964. The routes from Leith and Granton had ceased some time before that.

A ferry service to Kirkcaldy ran for a time in the early 1990s. In 2007 a hovercraft service between Portobello and Kirkcaldy was trialled. It was not taken up and there is currently no ferry crossing between Fife and Edinburgh and the Lothians.

CROSSING THE FORTH – BY RAIL

It's an icon recognised round the world, one of the highpoints of Scotland's genius for engineering, and the country's largest A-listed building. The Forth Rail Bridge is the acme of railway bridges.

When the bridge was officially opened in 1890, His Royal Highness Edward, the Prince of Wales, supposedly hammered in a rivet made of gold. However, financial strictures meant that the rivet was actually constructed of brass – and painted to look like gold.

Sixty-three men lost their lives during the seven-year construction of the bridge, and around 500 workmen were injured. Rescue boats moored in the Forth saved a further eight men from drowning. A persistent myth states that when some workmen were trapped at the foot of a cantilever and could not be rescued, they were put out of their misery when the authorities sent down food that had been secretly poisoned. This story is entirely fanciful.

The bridge has a surface area of 45 acres (18 hectares). For over 100 years 'Forth Bridge Red', created by the Edinburgh paint firm Craig & Rose, was applied continuously to the steelwork in a never-ending, year-round operation. 'It's like painting Forth Bridge', meaning a task that never ends, was once indeed based in truth, but advances in paint technology have changed all that, and now, although painting the underside of the deck will still take ten years, the paint will not need to be replaced for another two decades.

Another story that can be discounted is the oft-repeated statement that the first air raid of the Second World War was aimed at the Forth Bridge. The target was actually the Royal Navy ships in the Forth, and the German aircrews were specifically ordered to avoid attacking both the bridge and civilian areas.

The Forth Bridge appears in both 1935 and 1959 versions of the film *The Thirty-Nine Steps*, where the hero Richard Hannay (played by Robert Donat and Kenneth More respectively) stages a dramatic escape from a moving train into the waters of the Forth.

Iain Banks' extraordinary 1986 novel *The Bridge* is partly set on a fantasy version of the Forth Bridge, where an entire dystopian society lives amidst the vast steel superstructure.

If a Royal Navy vessel is passing under the bridge while a train is crossing, tradition demands that the navigating officer has to buy drinks for all the ship's officers. If two trains are crossing in opposite directions, however, it is the ship's captain who has to stand a round for all members of the crew.

CROSSING THE FORTH – BY ROAD

The dream of a permanent crossing of the Forth at Queensferry has had a long genesis. A tunnel was suggested in 1805, while the first design for a bridge appeared in 1818. These and other proposals were not taken up because of the financial crisis caused by the Napoleonic Wars.

In the 1930s two local businessmen energetically promoted the idea of a barrage dam with a road running along the top. It too came to nothing.

The current Forth Road Bridge was first proposed in the 1940s. It opened in 1964.

When the bridge was built it was the fourth longest suspension bridge in the world, and was nicknamed 'The Highway in the Sky'. Comparisons with San Francisco's Golden Gate Bridge are valid, although the Californian bridge has rather less in the way of dreich weather.

Even though the dedicated cycle lanes are separate from the traffic, cycling across the bridge in bad weather is not for the faint-hearted.

Like all suspension bridges, the Forth Road Bridge is designed to flex with the wind, and in the very strongest gales can move up to 25ft horizontally. As the overall structure compensates, motorists rarely notice the movement. In addition, if the air temperature soars, the central point of the bridge lowers very slightly.

In its first year of operation, 1,440,910 vehicles used the bridge. The bridge was designed for a maximum annual capacity of 11 million vehicles; a figure which, it was thought, would hardly ever be reached. Currently well over double that number cross per year, leading to issues of congestion and future structural integrity.

The bridge has had to be endlessly strengthened to cope with escalating numbers and the increased average weight of heavy goods vehicles.

In August 2011, 2,393,190 vehicles used the bridge, the highest monthly figure ever. On one day alone, Friday the 5th, 88,559 cars, motorcycles, van and lorries crossed.

After many years of wrangling, construction commenced in 2011 on the Forth Replacement Crossing, a new road bridge to the west of the existing bridges.

Some proposals for the new crossing suggested a tunnel. Although no road tunnel has ever been built under the Forth, a long-forgotten route deep under the river was opened in 1964. It linked the workings of Low Valleyfield Colliery on the south coast of Fife with Kinneil Colliery near Bo'Ness in West Lothian. Thousands of tons of coal moved south under the river, transported by inclined planes (Kinneil was much deeper than Low Valleyfield) and narrow-gauge electric railway. Both collieries were abandoned in the late 1970s and early 1980s, and the tunnel link closed.

BUSES

Unlike the majority of British cities, Edinburgh has resisted wholesale bus privatisation or sell-off and still has a bus company owned by the local authority. Lothian Buses, which operates the vast majority of buses within the city, is the only remaining municipal bus company in Scotland (there are also two in Wales and eight in England).

Lothian's Seafield depot is one of the locations for the CBeebies children's television programme *Me Too!*, produced by the makers of the successful *Balamory*. The inhabitants of the fictional city of Riverseafingal – created using CGI footage of Edinburgh and several other UK cities – get around by Riversea Buses.

During the Second World War, shortages of diesel saw nine single-decker buses converted to gas power, the gas held in huge ungainly bags in a trailer towed behind the bus.

In 1941, with many men called up, the buses were forced to introduce female conductors. At first, the conductresses were only employed on single-decker buses so that their stockinged legs could not be ogled when going up the stairs of double-deckers. This rule was later relaxed.

FLIGHT

Edinburgh was the location of the very first manned balloon flight in Britain. On 27 August 1784 James Tytler took off from Comely Garden, Abbeyhill, and landed half a mile away in Restalrig, having achieved a maximum height of 350ft. Tytler was a man for whom

the phrase 'glorious failure' could have been invented: although a brilliant chemist full of ideas and a prolific writer, most of his subsequent schemes, including several additional balloon attempts, were abject flops, and he spent his life bedevilled by a lack of both money and success.

'Balloon' Tytler is said to have inspired the Scottish vernacular term for fool or idiot, as in 'you're a balloon.'

The unlucky Tytler was elbowed out of the ballooning limelight by Italian Vincenzo Lunardi, whose well-publicised flights across Europe and England ensured a massive turnout (perhaps 80,000 strong) for his first Edinburgh venture on 5 October 1785. Taking off from Heriot's Hospital (now George Heriot's School) south of the Grassmarket, Lunardi flew 40 miles across the Forth to the Fife town of Ceres. Two subsequent flights from Edinburgh ended up (1) over Arthur's Seat and (2) in the cold waters of the Forth off Gullane in East Lothian.

The balloonist's adventures inspired songs such as 'Lunardi's Gone Up to the Moon', as well as making their mark on female fashion, with balloon motifs woven into both outer and inner garments, while ludicrous balloon-like 'Lunardi' hats made their appearance on Edinburgh's High Street. It was perhaps no coincidence that the flamboyant Italian 'fly-boy' had a passionate female fan-base.

The first direct flight between Britain and the USA took place on 2 July 1919, when Airship R.34 left East Fortune airfield, 20 miles east of Edinburgh, for New York. On board for the eleven-day journey were thirty crew, two carrier pigeons, an adventure-seeking aircraftman who had stowed away the night before, and Wopsie the tabby kitten, who had been smuggled onboard as the flight's unofficial mascot.

On 15 June 1928, as part of a publicity stunt, a race from London to Edinburgh was organised between an Imperial Airways Argosy airliner, taking off from Croydon Aerodrome, and the record-breaking locomotive *The Flying Scotsman*. The plane should have won easily, but pilot Gordon Olley diverted to Norfolk to wave at some relatives who were staying on a houseboat, and by the time his passengers had disembarked at Turnhouse and travelled into the city to Waverley Station, the train had already arrived.

In 1928 Sir Alan Cobham touched down in Leith's western harbour as part of a round-Britain flight in his flying boat. Many years later, in 1950, Leith docks became a certified flying boat airport. Sadly the

Greenock-Leith-Southampton route was not commercially viable and Aquila Airways withdrew the service after just a month. The Leith Dock Commission, however, continued to renew the one guinea licence fee every year in the hope that a company would return to the harbour. The licence fee was last paid in 1959, by which point there were no commercial flying boats left.

Edinburgh Airport grew out of the First and Second World War airfield of RAF Turnhouse, west of the city. The first commercial service to London flew in 1947.

In 1977 the inadequate facilities at Turnhouse were entirely replaced with a new runway and a terminal further to the west, while the original site became the cargo and small parcels hub. This 'cargo village' is now the busiest in Scotland and the third busiest mail operation in the UK.

The landmark pepperpot of the Air Traffic Control Tower is 187ft (57m) high.

Edinburgh Airport has its own fire service, which is operational 24/7.

Fog affects the airport on average eight days a year.

The airport is Scotland's busiest and is currently the sixth largest airport in the UK in terms of passenger numbers. Around 9 million people arrive and depart each year. About 4,000 people work at the airport, of whom just over 10 per cent actually work *for* the airport.

4

WARS, BATTLES AND RIOTS

AGES DARK AND DEADLY

One of the oldest poems in British literature commemorates the vast slaughter visited by the Angles of Northumbria on the Kingdom of Gododdin, whose base was Dun Eidyn – Edinburgh. *Y Gododdin* tells how in about AD 603 the warriors and allies of Mynyddog the Wealthy feasted in a great hall atop what is now Castle Hill, before heading out to bloody defeat at Catterick in Yorkshire. The Gododdin were Britons, a Celtic people who spoke a form of Welsh, and the poem was composed in Welsh by Aneirin, Mynyddog's court bard, one of the few survivors of the battle.

Castle Rock's defensive position, on a hill surrounded by cliffs on three sides, was a natural fortress, and inevitably changed hands numerous times during the Dark Ages. Britons, Angles, Picts, Danes and the Scots (who came from Ireland) all fought over the site.

MEDIEVAL MAYHEM

In the Middle Ages, possession of Castle Rock swung between the Scots and the English numerous times. On more than one occasion – as under the orders of Robert the Bruce in 1314 – the occupiers actually destroyed the castle, to prevent it being used by the enemy.

Edinburgh's most important battle was fought nowhere near the city. A Scottish invasion of England culminated in the Battle of Flodden Field in Northumberland, which saw the Scots army utterly annihilated on 9 September 1513. Amongst the 10,000 dead were King James IV and hundreds of nobles, creating a political and leadership crisis that damaged Scotland for a generation. In Edinburgh the aftermath of the slaughter saw the hasty construction of the Flodden Wall, a defence against the English (whose expected invasion did not materialise). The wall only succeeded in hemming in Edinburgh's citizens for well over two centuries, thus creating one of the densest urban populations in Europe.

Flodden is now part of the patriotic mythology of Scotland, being commemorated in the well-known lament and pipe tune *The Flowers of the Forest.*

Great battles create their own folklore. Many Scots, unable to comprehend the scale of the disaster, clung to the mistaken belief that the king had survived. Elsewhere, it was reported that the names of all those of noble birth who had died had been read out in advance of the battle at Edinburgh's Mercat Cross on the Royal Mile, the standard place for official proclamations. The herald in this case was a being called Plotcock, a Scottish version of the name Pluto, that is, Satan. Richard Lawson, upon hearing the Summons of Plotcock, threw a crown coin at the demon to appeal against the sentence of death. Of all the gentlemen on the list, Lawson alone survived. Or so the story goes.

The Boar Stone, where the Royal Standard was last pitched for the muster of the Scottish army before Flodden, sits on a wall on Morningside Road.

THE WARS OF MARY, QUEEN OF SCOTS

Sixteenth-century Scotland was caught between the two competing powers of England and France. For both countries the prize in the 1540s was a dynastic marriage with the heir to the throne of Scotland – Mary, Queen of Scots. The fact that Mary was an infant was irrelevant, as both the prince-candidates of France and England were themselves small children. What mattered was the marriage contract. Henry VIII of England tried to bully the Scots into submission in the 'War of the Rough Wooing', during which much of Edinburgh was put to the torch in 1544. He didn't succeed, and Mary sailed to France.

In 1560 the 'Auld Alliance' between Catholic France and newly-Protestant Scotland splintered, and French troops found themselves besieged in Leith by their previous allies the Scots. Who were in turn assisted by *their* new allies – the English.

During a brief break in the siege, French and English soldiers ate together on the beach at Leith. The English had beef, bacon, poultry, wine and beer, but the best the French could manage was horse pie and roast rat. It was a sign of how desperate things had become behind the fortified ramparts of Leith. Unable to fight any longer, after six months the French surrendered and were honourably evacuated to Calais.

Less than two months later, Mary, Queen of Scots, newly widowed and abandoned by a France that no longer needed her, arrived in a devastated Leith.

The next few tumultuous years featured some of the most infamous scenes in Scottish history. Mary, pregnant, was attacked in Holyrood Palace. Her secretary David Rizzio was murdered in front of her by a party led by her second husband Lord Darnley. Darnley himself was assassinated at Kirk O'Field, the site of the current university – a still-mysterious murder in which Mary may or may not have been implicated. Mary was married (forcibly or otherwise) to the Earl of Bothwell, who had probably killed Darnley. And Mary was eventually forced to flee Scotland, her fate imprisonment and execution in an English castle.

From 1571 to 1573, with Mary in exile, her supporters held Edinburgh Castle. The resulting two-year siege – which saw terror tactics such as the poisoning of wells and the burning of occupied houses – was eventually broken when more than 3,000 cannonballs were fired at the castle. So great was the destruction that the vast majority of the castle had to be rebuilt from scratch.

THE COVENANTERS AND THE CIVIL WARS

The great struggles of the seventeenth century often focused on matters of religion – not between Catholic and Protestant, but between different flavours of Protestantism. In 1638 Scottish Presbyterians, resisting the Anglican impositions of King Charles I, signed a National Covenant stating their allegiance to their religious principles. Over the next few decades these Covenanters fought a bitter civil war against three successive kings, which saw yet another siege of Edinburgh Castle (the Royalist garrison was forced to surrender after three months).

Around 18,000 Covenanters were killed for their beliefs. Edinburgh became a factory of death, as Covenanters were hanged and dismembered, their heads and limbs displayed on spikes as a warning to others.

In 1679 Edinburgh invented the concentration camp, herding 1,200 Covenanter prisoners into an open enclosure in Greyfriars Kirkyard and leaving many of them to die of exposure or starvation.

The religious wars in Scotland inevitably spilled over into the English Civil Wars. The period was characterised by prominent men frequently changing sides. At one point the Scottish Presbyterians fought on the same side as Cromwell's Parliamentarians. When the Scots' allegiance changed, Cromwell's forces invaded Scotland, leading to Edinburgh being under English occupation for almost ten years.

THE JACOBITE WARS

The first Jacobite Rising of 1689 saw yet another siege of the castle, this one lasting three months before the Jacobite defenders surrendered for lack of water. At one point the garrison, sheltering from the cannonade in deep shelters, became so bored they sent a message to the attackers asking for a pack of playing cards. Most unsportingly, the request was refused.

The 1715 Rising found the Jacobites occupying Leith for just one night, then hustling out of the way before a pursuing Government army turned up. The Jacobites left with thirty new recruits, two of whom were later captured and hanged for rebellion.

In 1745 Edinburgh offered no resistance to Bonnie Prince Charlie's then-unbeaten Jacobite army, and the 'Young Pretender' enjoyed a sociable occupation of Holyrood Palace. Despite the prince's undeniable glamour, however, Edinburgh couldn't get very excited about the Jacobite cause. No one resisted, but no one joined up, either, and what was a major conflict elsewhere in Scotland was largely greeted with an indifferent shrug by most of the city's inhabitants. With the tactics and technology of warfare changing, Edinburgh's role as a locus for battles and sieges was finally at an end.

RIOT!

Penned up in their cramped and walled city and beset by hardship and misery, the poor of Edinburgh's filthy streets and overcrowded tenements frequently came together as a vicious and volatile mob, often for the slightest of reasons. When powered by a semi-political agenda, however, the mob was fearsome enough to frighten anyone in authority. Here are some of the city's key riots:

1561 The new Protestant regime attempted to ban the traditional street plays performed by craftsmen and apprentices, and condemned

one man to death as a 'ringleader'. The mob rescued the fellow, smashed the gallows, and terrorised the magistrates.

1682   The naval press-gang was justifiably hated. When a group of popular young men were 'pressed', a riot kicked off. Soldiers shot and killed between ten and twelve people, causing the violence to spill over into the following day.

1707   The Edinburgh mob detested the idea of Union with England. Those Scottish aristocrats intending to sign the Act of Union were pursued through the streets, eventually being forced to seek shelter in a cellar in the High Street (other signatures were added in a garden behind Moray House). The signatories notoriously sold their votes, Lord Banff wanting a mere £11 2s 0d, while the Duke of Queensberry, the Lord High Commissioner, demanded £12,325. The proceedings inspired Robert Burns to pen his famous lines, 'We are bought and sold for English gold / Such a parcel of rogues in a nation!'

1736   Some in the huge crowd at a public execution started throwing stones at the hangman. The City Guard opened fire, killing at least six and injuring many others, most of whom were not involved in the affray. Captain John Porteous of the City Guard was convicted over the killings, sentenced to death, and then reprieved. The incensed mob stormed the Tolbooth and lynched Porteous from a street sign in the Grassmarket.

1779   Anti-Catholic rioters burned and looted Catholic houses and a chapel; the City Guard not only stood back and let things happen, they accepted on-the-spot bribes to unlock doors for easier looting.

1792   Troops opened fire on a demonstration agitating for parliamentary reform. There was at least one fatality, and the rioting continued into a second day.

1811   A Hogmanay orgy of drunken violence and robbery on the Royal Mile resulted in two citizens being beaten to death, plus numerous other assaults and attacks on property. One of the dead was a police officer. Three young men were hanged for the murders, while others were transported to the penal colonies in Australia.

1823   During a time of anti-Irish feeling prompted by mass Irish immigration, the bakers of Edinburgh and Leith and the colliers of Musselburgh squared up against Irish punters at Musselburgh Races. There were no deaths, but numerous injuries.

1935   Another anti-Catholic riot, this time under the direction of the far-right group Protestant Action.

2005   The G8 meeting of world leaders at Auchterarder in Perthshire saw a successive series of protests held in Edinburgh, ranging from the peaceful 200,000-plus 'Make Poverty History' march, to later, much smaller and periodically violent demonstrations which brought the city centre to a standstill.

FIGHTING MEN

In April 1779 the gulf between old and new Scotland came into vivid focus. Gaelic-speaking recruits from the Highlands were due to disembark from Leith to fight against the American rebels, when they were told they were to be transferred to a Lowland, English-speaking regiment. As part of this transfer they were to abandon the kilt and wear breeks (trousers). The Highlanders refused to comply, largely because the terms of their signing-up had expressly stated they would only serve in a Highland regiment. When troops were dispatched from Edinburgh Castle to enforce the ruling, the Gaelic-speaking Highlanders, unable to understand the orders shouted at them in English, responded with violence. Ten soldiers were killed and thirty-one injured. Three of the Highlanders were found guilty of mutiny and murder, but granted an immediate pardon, and thereafter they and the remainder of the mutineers served loyally in their designated Highland regiment.

Dean Cemetery marks the final resting place of one of the most extraordinary soldiers of the Victorian age: Major General Sir Hector Archibald MacDonald. In contrast to the vast majority of army officers, who were upper class, 'Fighting Mac' was a crofter's son who had started as a private and risen to the rank of general through his own abilities, which included iron courage and a mastery of battle tactics. After a stellar career he became a national hero in 1898 for his actions at the Battle of Omdurman in Sudan. Five years later MacDonald shot himself over a homosexual scandal. His funeral in Edinburgh, supposedly a secret because of the Government's embarrassment, was attended by 30,000 mourners.

THE VICTORIA CROSS

The Victoria Cross is the highest honour in the British armed forces, and is presented for acts of exceptional bravery. It was first awarded in 1857, following the carnage of the Crimean War against Russia.

Nine former pupils of the Edinburgh Academy have been awarded the VC, three during the Indian Mutiny of 1857–58:

Lieutenant (later Colonel) Thomas Cadell of the 2nd European Bengal Fusiliers, who rescued two men under withering enemy fire.

Lieutenant (later Lieutenant General) Sir James Hills-Johnes of the Bengal Horse Artillery, who won his VC for conspicuous bravery at the Siege of Delhi.

Lieutenant (later Lieutenant General) John Adam Tytler of the Bengal Native Infantry, who was thrice wounded during desperate hand-to-hand combat.

Other former pupils from Edinburgh Academy so honoured include Lieutenant (later Captain) James Dundas of the Bengal Engineers (Bhutan, 1865); Captain (later Major) John Cook of the Bengal Staff Corps (Afghanistan, 1879); and Major (later Colonel) Edward Douglas Browne-Synge-Hutchinson of the 14th Hussars (South Africa, 1900).

During the First World War, another former pupil, Lieutenant (later Major) Allan Ebenezer Ker of the Gordon Highlanders, was awarded the Victoria Cross for holding 500 Germans at bay during a fierce engagement near St Quentin in France. And in the Second World War submariner Lieutenant Commander (later Rear Admiral) Anthony Cecil Chapel Miers earned a VC for actions off Corfu.

The service ranks of the former Edinburgh Academy pupils necessarily reflect their status in society. Other Edinburgh recipients of the Victoria Cross come from a wider diversity of social backgrounds. They include:

During the Crimean War:

1854, Alma, Crimea: Private William Reynolds of the Scots Guards, who received his VC at the very first ceremony performed by Queen Victoria, which took place in 1857. He was the first man of the rank of private to be awarded the VC.

1854, Balaclava, Crimea: Sergeant Henry Ramage of the Royal Scots Greys. His VC is on display at the Royal Scots Dragoon Guards Museum at Edinburgh Castle.

1855, Sebastopol, Crimea: Lieutenant (later Colonel) William Hope of the 7th Regiment of Foot.

During the Indian Mutiny:

1858, Fort Ruhya, India: Private James Davis of the 42nd Regiment (Black Watch). His full name was James Davis Kelly but he dropped the 'Kelly' when he enlisted because of anti-Irish prejudice. His memorial is in North Merchiston Cemetery.

1858, Fort Ruhya, India: Quartermaster-Sergeant (later Major) John Simpson of the 42nd Regiment (Black Watch).

1858, Fort Ruhya, India: Lance-Corporal Alexander Thompson, the third member of the Black Watch to receive the VC at this engagement.

During the Opium Wars:

1860, Taku Forts, China: Private John Leishman McDougall of the 44th Regiment. His memorial is in Old Calton Cemetery.

During the Boer War:

1900, Dewetsdorp, South Africa: Private Charles Thomas Kennedy of the Highland Light Infantry. His memorial is in North Merchiston Cemetery.

1900, Johannesburg, South Africa: Lance-Corporal (later Lieutenant Colonel) John Fredrick Mackay of the Gordon Highlanders.

1900, Krugersdorp, South Africa: Captain David Reginald Younger of the Gordon Highlanders. He died during the battle.

1900, Ladysmith, South Africa: Lieutenant Robert James Thomas Digby-Jones of the Corps of Royal Engineers, posthumously awarded the VC for his part in the defence of Wagon Hill during the siege of Ladysmith.

During the First World War:
1914, Verneuill, France: Private George Wilson of the Highland Light Infantry. His memorial is in Piershill Cemetery.

1914, Becelaere, Belgium: Captain Walter Lorrain Brodie of the Highland Light Infantry.

1914, Givenchy, France: Lieutenant William Arthur McCrae Bruce of the Indian Army. He was awarded the medal posthumously.

1914, Missy, France: Captain William Henry Johnston of the Corps of Royal Engineers.

1914, Dar-es-Salaam Harbour, Tanzania: Captain Henry Peel Ritchie RN. His memorial is in Warriston Cemetery.

1916, Mlali, Tanzania: Captain William Anderson Bloomfield of the 2nd South African Mounted Brigade.

1918, Hoogemolen, Belgium: Lieutenant David Stuart McGregor of the Royal Scots. His Victoria Cross, awarded posthumously, is on display in the Royal Scots Museum in Edinburgh Castle.

1918, Aubencheul-au-Bac, France: Corporal James McPhie of the Corps of Royal Engineers. His VC was awarded posthumously.

1918, Ors, France: Sapper Adam Archibald of the Corps of Field Engineers, who built a floating bridge across a canal under intense fire, just a week before the Armistice. His memorial is in Warriston Cemetery.

During the Second World War:
1945, Lake Comacchio, Italy: Corporal Thomas Peck Hunter of the Royal Marines. His posthumous medal is (to date) the last VC

awarded to a member of the Marines. His memorial can be seen on Britannia Walk in Leith.

The Royal Scots Museum in the castle also holds the Victoria Crosses for five other heroes of the First World War – Corporal Robert Dunsire, Major Roland Edward Elcock, Private Hugh McIver, Captain Henry Reynolds, and Private Henry Howey Robson – and one from the Crimean War, Private Joseph Prosser.

The National War Museum of Scotland at the castle holds eleven Victoria Crosses won by Scottish servicemen from the Crimean War to the Korean War:

Private John Alexander (1855)
Sergeant Major Cornelius Coughlan (1857)
Surgeon Valentine Munbee McMaster (1857)
Private Duncan Millar (1859)
Lieutenant Colonel William Robertson (1899)
Lance Corporal William Angus (1915)
Sergeant Piper Daniel Logan Laidlaw (1915)
Sergeant John Brown Hamilton (1917)
Lieutenant David Lowe MacIntyre (1918)
Flight Sergeant George Thompson (1945)
Sergeant William Speakman (1951)

THE FIRST WORLD WAR

On the declaration of war in August 1914, two German cargo ships, the *Otto* and the *Adolf*, were immediately seized in Leith Dock.

The first sinking of a Royal Navy vessel in the war happened at the entrance to the Forth. The cruiser HMS *Pathfinder* was torpedoed by a U-boat on 5 September 1914; all but nine of the crew died.

The Firth remained a danger zone for the rest of the war, with numerous vessels lost to U-boats, mines and the occasional collision with friendly vessels. On 31 January 1917 two British submarines were sunk and three others damaged in a 'pile-up' with Royal Navy surface ships. One hundred men drowned or were mown down in the dark by the ships which did not know the submariners were struggling in the water. The wrecks of submarines *K4* and *K17* have never been raised and remain deep below the waters off the Isle of May.

In 1908 author Neil Munro had written a 'science fiction' story for the Glasgow *Evening News* in which he imagined the German Zeppelins attacking Rosyth naval base and the Forth Bridge. Although events did not turn out exactly as Munro had predicted, Edinburgh was indeed bombed – because a Zeppelin navigator mistook Leith Docks for the intended target, Rosyth Naval Base on the other side of the Forth.

Four Zeppelins set out from Germany on the night of Sunday, 2 April 1916. One got lost, one dropped its bombs over rural Northumberland, and a third caused superficial damage on the very edge of the city. It was the Imperial German Navy Zeppelin *L14*, commanded by Kapitänleutnant Aloys Böcker, which dropped twenty-four bombs, killing thirteen people, injuring twenty-four, and causing millions of pounds' worth of damage. The bombing is vividly commemorated in one of the stained-glass windows in the Scottish National War Memorial at Edinburgh Castle.

The Zeppelin first attacked the docks and then followed the reflective surface of the Water of Leith towards the city centre.

The National Museum of Flight at East Fortune, 20 miles east of Edinburgh, has one of the unexploded bombs from the raid, complete with the handles that show the high-explosive or incendiary weapons were simply dropped by hand.

Edinburgh was almost entirely unprepared for the air raid. No anti-aircraft guns were fired. The famous One O'Clock Gun at the castle did fire – but its blank ammunition was hardly going to bring down the enemy. A lone Royal Flying Corps fighter, an Avro 504 biplane, took off from East Fortune airfield, but could not locate the Zeppelins in the dark, and crashed on landing. The pilot was badly injured.

Edinburgh was thereafter protected by a ring of Royal Flying Corps fighters at East Fortune, Drem and Turnhouse. Short-lived military airfields were also established in Colinton and Gilmerton.

On 21 November 1918, thirty-four vessels of the German Navy steamed into the Firth of Forth for the official surrender. A massive part of the British fleet accompanied the battleships and battlecruisers to an anchorage off Inchkeith, while two Scottish-based airships hovered overhead.

The end of the First World War also saw the German Ocean renamed as the North Sea.

THE SECOND WORLD WAR

On Friday, 1 September 1939, two days before the official declaration of war, the Scottish Crown Jewels were taken from the Crown Room in Edinburgh Castle and secured in an underground vault, protected behind a layer of sandbags and a locked fireproof door. On 12 May 1942 further precautions were taken – the regalia were relocated into a pair of zinc-lined cases, one of which was hidden deep inside a shaft in Tank Room No. 1 under the Half Moon Battery, while the second was buried beneath the floor of a nearby room.

At the same time, the most precious items in the National Gallery of Scotland were secreted in a secure site in Innerleithen, in the Scottish Borders.

Goebbels, the Nazi propaganda minister, thought that Edinburgh was so delightful it would make a suitable summer capital when Britain became part of Hitler's empire.

A number of rich and influential people in 1930s Britain expressed virulently anti-Jewish and pro-Nazi sentiments. Among these was Captain Archibald Maule Ramsay, the Conservative MP for Peebles and South Midlothian. In 1939 Ramsay formed the Right Club, a secret fascist society. On 20 May 1940 MI5 and Special Branch arrested Ramsay and other Right Club members in London, and Ramsay spent four years in jail. Other members of the Right Club included Sir Samuel Chapman, Conservative MP for Edinburgh South, who had campaigned to exclude Jewish refugees escaping the Nazis from entering Britain. Meanwhile, Professor A.P. Laurie, an expert on the chemistry of oil paintings and principal of Heriot-Watt College, was a vocal member of the pro-Nazi organisation The Link, which published the rabidly anti-Semitic *Anglo-German Review.*

When Italy entered the war in 1940, dozens of Italian-owned premises in Edinburgh and beyond were smashed up and looted. Although some of the victims were known fascists – such as the Stockbridge chip shop proprietor who was often seen in his Blackshirt uniform – anti-Italian feeling was so intense that indiscriminate violence was also meted out to those who had no interest in Mussolini.

THE FIRST AIR RAID OF THE WAR

The city had two military airfields. 603 (City of Edinburgh) Squadron was based at RAF Turnhouse (now Edinburgh Airport). 602 (City of Glasgow) Squadron, meanwhile, was based at RAF Drem near North Berwick in East Lothian. Both were part of the Auxiliary Air Force, the RAF equivalent of the part-time Territorial Army, and their 'weekend pilots' had just taken delivery of brand-new Spitfires. The hastily-constructed masts at Drone Hill, on the coast between Dunbar and Eyemouth, provided radar information to Fighter Command's command and control network at Turnhouse. In the early days of the war both the human and technological parts of this network were untested, leading to several mistakes.

The first air raid on the British Isles took place on 16 October 1939. That day, the Drone Hill radar station broke down (an electrical valve had blown), and plotting errors at Turnhouse led to the RAF fighters being first sent in the wrong directions.

The first German bomber was sighted flying up the Forth at 1427 hours – but it took eleven minutes before the order was given for the anti-aircraft batteries to open fire, by which time the first bombs had already been dropped.

The bombers were aiming for the Royal Navy ships sheltering in the Forth. Having failed to find his primary target HMS *Hood* – in contrast to the belief of German intelligence, the great battlecruiser was not in Rosyth that day – Hauptman Helmut Pohle decided to bomb two cruisers moored off South Queensferry. As the Junkers JU 88 went into a steep dive, the cockpit canopy snapped off, taking the rear top gun with it. Hauptman Pohle completed the attack with the wind screaming in his eyes. Not surprisingly, he missed.

Other bombers that day were more successful. A bomb smacked right through the cruiser HMS *Southampton*, exiting above the waterline, and her sister cruiser HMS *Edinburgh* was slightly damaged. The casualties on the two warships were relatively slight – ten injuries in total. But off the Fife coast the destroyer HMS *Mohawk* suffered major damage and sixteen lives were lost. Commander Jolly, despite being severely wounded, brought his ship safely into Rosyth. He died hours later, and was posthumously awarded the George Cross.

Once the initial shock had worn off, both anti-aircraft and naval guns opened up from every quarter, and the Spitfires, having returned from their wild goose chase, engaged the bombers, leading to chases at roof-top height across Edinburgh and the countryside. Red-hot shrapnel and unexploded shells from the anti-aircraft barrage cascaded down over the streets, accompanied by the thousands of bullets fired by the Spitfire pilots. This rain of metal led to Edinburgh's first war casualty – painter Joe McLuskie, who was hit in the abdomen by a Spitfire bullet while working at a house in Portobello. He survived an emergency operation at Leith Hospital. John Ferry in West Pilton was also wounded by the Spitfires, this time in the leg. Several other less serious injuries were reported from Kirkliston and Davidson's Mains. Across the city windows were smashed and furniture and ornaments destroyed, telephone wires were cut, and a tram was hit, while many people had close shaves, and one woman found a bullet in her baby's pram.

One of the machine-gunners in action at Turnhouse airfield that day was the padre of 603 Squadron, the Revd Rossie Brown. When upbraided for only having fired a short burst at an overflying bomber, the padre replied, 'Yes, it passed too quickly out of my diocese!'

By the end of the day, the RAF fighters had downed two bombers and damaged another one. One JU 88 came down off Port Seton in East Lothian, the three surviving crew being picked up from the water by a fishing yawl. In gratitude, Oberleutnant Hans Storp, the pilot, gave skipper John Dickson a gold ring, which is still a treasured family heirloom. Hauptman Pohle, meanwhile, who had led the very first attack on the UK, was downed off the coast of Fife. Although wounded, he was the only one of his crew to survive. In all, four Luftwaffe personnel had been killed, the bodies of two being recovered and buried in Portobello Cemetery.

As well as the problems with radar and inaccurate plotting of positions, no siren had been sounded to warn the civilian population. Commands had been sluggish, uncoordinated and inaccurate. A train had been given permission to cross the Forth Bridge right in the middle of the attack, giving the passengers a grandstand view of the mêlée. Meanwhile, Sea Skua training planes from Donibristle airfield had been in the air throughout the raid, getting in everyone's way and sometimes being mistaken for German bombers. Two Spitfires had almost collided in mid-air, while the pilots had yet to get used to the way their planes kicked downwards when they used their guns, so most of the more than 20,000 rounds fired that day had missed. In addition, their training procedures had been designed for outmoded biplanes. To make matters worse, Royal Navy ships had sometimes fired at RAF aircraft (a similar problem with friendly fire had occurred on 27 September, when fighters from the City of Edinburgh Squadron were fired upon by the destroyer HMS *Valorous*, whom they were supposed to be protecting).

The baptism of fire known as the Forth Raid was a wake-up call for Edinburgh's air defence network. Even by 1941, however, sirens often went off *after* the attacks started. And 'All Clear' sirens would sometimes sound while raids were still in progress – as evidenced by bombs continuing to fall.

The two Spitfire pilots who had scored the kills on 16 October, Flight Lieutenant Patrick 'Patsy' Gifford of the City of Edinburgh Squadron and George Pinkerton of the City of Glasgow Squadron, were each awarded the Distinguished Flying Cross for their efforts. The raid was recreated for the British propaganda film *Squadron 992*, with a RAF Blenheim playing the part of Hans Storp's Junkers 88. As skipper John Dickson was being filmed in a reconstruction of his rescue of the German crew from the Forth, he and the camera crew were promptly arrested on suspicion of being spies.

THE WAR IN THE AIR

The first anti-aircraft barrage balloon was flown over the Forth on 18 October 1939 – two days after the Forth Raid.

Some of the barrage balloons were attached to ships moored in the river. On 6 July 1940 twelve balloons were destroyed by a thunderstorm.

On 21 December 1939 the problem with 'friendly fire' became lethal. In atrocious, low-visibility conditions, 602 Squadron shot down two of what they thought were German Dorniers – only to discover their kills were the similarly-shaped RAF Hampden bombers. One of the Hampden crewmen was drowned. The Spitfire pilots were exonerated at the Court of Inquiry the following day, when it was revealed the Hampdens were way off course and had not extended their undercarriages, the standard signal that they were not enemy 'bogeys'.

In 1941 two Spitfires on a training exercise collided above Edinburgh. One of the aircraft plummeted to earth, the pilot's parachute failing to open. In September 2010 the remains of the crashed fighter plane were unearthed in Edinburgh's Royal Botanic Gardens.

The early part of the war saw a series of aerial bombing and strafing attacks on trawlers from Granton, with the *Isabelle Greig* and *River*

Earn being sunk and the *Compagnus* and *Eileen Wray* damaged. Many similar engagements involving Forth trawlers were to follow. The *Isabelle Greig* was the ship featured in the pioneering short film *Granton Trawler*, made in 1934 by John Grierson, 'Father of the Documentary'.

The strategic intention of the Luftwaffe at this stage was to close the Forth to the Royal Navy, as well as to disrupt the North Sea convoys. However, so successful were the RAF fighters from Turnhouse, Drem and the other east coast airfields, that the Firth of Forth was soon nicknamed 'Suicide Corner' by the German aircrews.

603 (City of Edinburgh) Squadron, in conjunction with the 602 (City of Glasgow) Squadron, scored another success on 28 October 1939 when they caused a Heinkel 111 bomber to crash land near Humbie in East Lothian. This was one of the first enemy aircraft to crash on British soil, and was pored over by intelligence officers, who found documents describing Royal Navy ships, as well as quantities of hard biscuits, corned beef, and German sausage. One of the Heinkel's engines was taken to Rolls-Royce, where the quality of the engineering was assessed as being of the highest order.

At 0105 hours on 26 June 1940 a Spitfire from 603 Squadron brought down another Heinkel. This was only the second time a Spitfire had successfully attacked an enemy aircraft at night – the first having occurred just forty minutes earlier, off the Yorkshire coast.

The first civilian casualties as a result of direct enemy action came on 18 July 1940, when ten bombs were dropped on Leith, killing seven people in George Street.

Raids over the Edinburgh area, never heavy when compared to other cities, were reduced further when the principal focus of the air war shifted to the south of England for the summer of 1940 – the Battle of Britain.

The Battle of Britain saw the City of Edinburgh Squadron move to London, where they lost twelve pilots and sixteen aircraft in just twelve days. The squadron returned to Turnhouse in December 1940.

When a bomb blast revealed the foundations of long-forgotten buildings in Holyrood Park, curious visitors had to pay one penny to see the result. The takings, about £300, went to the Spitfire Fund, which was used to build more Spitfires.

The penultimate raid on Edinburgh, on 25 March 1943, saw the West Pilton anti-aircraft battery shoot down three bombers. Then a full thirteen months passed before a single Junkers 88 appeared out of nowhere on 5 May 1944 and launched a brief low-level strafing attack. That was the last time Edinburgh saw the Luftwaffe.

In total, eighteen people were killed by bombs between 1940 and 1942, with more than 200 injured.

THE WAR AT SEA

On 21 October 1939 the new 6in cruiser HMS *Belfast* was badly damaged by a magnetic mine dropped into the Firth by a German aircraft. It took three years for the 10,500-ton warship to return to active service. Another mine annihilated the Naval Boom Defence Vessel *Bayonet* on 21 December, this mine bobbing up less than a mile from Leith Docks. For several years the Royal Navy minesweepers fought a battle of attrition against German mines, constantly having to sweep a safe channel through the Firth.

On 21 February 1940, when the Admiralty trawler *Peter Carey* was in danger of straying out of the safe mine-swept channel in the Forth, the gunners at Inchkeith Battery fired a practice shell across its bows. The warning had the desired effect, but the empty shell bounced off the surface of the water and smashed through a flat and garden shed on Salamander Street in Leith, 3.5 miles away. The round was returned to Inchkeith with a note that read: 'We believe this belongs to you.'

In 1940, after the Nazi occupation of Norway, Prince Olaf, the country's Crown Prince, set up the Norwegian government in exile in the Burgh Chambers at Queensferry. Each December the prince's loyal countrymen on the secret 'Shetland Bus' operation smuggled a Norwegian Fir across the North Sea so Olaf and his fellow naval officers could decorate it with Christmas candles as a reminder of their beleaguered homeland. After the war, Norway repaid Scotland's hospitality by gifting a Christmas tree to Edinburgh, a tradition which continues to this day.

Prince Olaf was just one of 17,000 men who were trained at the mine-sweeping school at Port Edgar near South Queensferry, the Royal Navy's only such facility in the UK. The school was known as HMS *Lochinvar* for the duration of the war.

The German submarine *U2336* torpedoed and sank the merchant vessels *Avondale Park* and the *Sneland I* off the Isle of May at the eastern edge of the Firth of Firth. The action took place at 11 p.m. on the 7 May 1945 – one hour before Germany officially surrendered. This entirely unnecessary attack, by a U-boat commander who had already been ordered to surrender by his own high command, was the final action of the war.

So, in 1939 the Forth saw the first attack on Britain; and six years later, it saw the last.

HOME DEFENCES

The 3rd Cavalry Training Regiment, based at Redford Barracks in Colinton, had not yet noticed that warfare had become mechanised: in 1939 they were still using horses while Hitler's Panzers were smashing through Europe.

The Local Defence Volunteers, or Home Guard, was founded in May 1940. At first, the Edinburgh force, deprived of any modern weapons, cobbled together a miscellany of old guns, some of which dated back to the Boer War.

Pillboxes were put up on key streets, such as on Shandwick Place, where the defensive nature of the structure outside the Rutland Hotel was disguised as a *faux* florist's shop.

Another pillbox appeared at the opposite end of Princes Street, at the junction with Waterloo Place. Here, however, the minimal attempt at camouflage featured just a couple of painted-on windows and corner columns.

In 1942 Edinburgh police conducted a survey of road accidents. Hastily-constructed blockhouses and pillboxes, by creating blind corners, had caused 155 accidents, fifty-five injuries and two deaths. The most dangerous blockhouse was the one at the corner of Lothian Road and Princes Street, which was responsible for no less than forty accidents.

Slit trenches were dug in the Meadows, Inverleith Park, Leith Links, Crewe Toll and the gardens of the city centre. Golf courses at Bruntsfield Links, Craigentinny, Craigieknowe and Cramond were festooned with obstacles designed to prevent them being used by enemy aircraft or gliders. As these obstacles included poles, trenches and railway sleepers, the golfers were not impressed.

The Scottish Command Camouflage School was at Ravelston Elms, while urban warfare was taught at abandoned tenements in East Cromwell Street in Leith and the wrecked whisky warehouse in Duff Street. Exercises took place on Arthur's Seat, the Braid Hills and around Cramond, some of which saw broken gates and fences, livestock carelessly liberated from fields, and citizens suffering the effects of mistakenly released tear gas.

One Home Guard battalion had its HQ in Holyrood Palace. After exercises in Holyrood Park, some of the resident sheep were found to have mysteriously disappeared.

A small French bistro appeared in Liberton in 1944. Madame Dubois' 'Estaminet des trios Roses' was in reality a mocked-up building where, in advance of the liberation of France, sappers were trained to search for and disarm booby-traps.

After D-Day the grounds of Gosford House near Longniddry became a prisoner of war camp for 3,000 captured Germans.

The Home Guard was disbanded in December 1944.

THE HOME FRONT

Edinburgh's planning for air-raid shelters started as early as 1938, but it was never enough. By October 1939, there were sufficient shelters for about 140,000 people, or one third of the population, and even then many of the shelters were barely adequate in terms of protection.

Large public shelters were constructed under the YMCA (St Andrew Square), Morrison's Garage (Roseburn Bridge) and St Stephen's Church (St Vincent Street) and in the subterranean storerooms of the Southern Cemetery. Large companies, such as British Rubber in Fountainbridge, used their own basements. Some commercial concerns tried to cash in on the demand for shelter space by charging the authorities outrageous rents for underground areas, which led to some much-needed shelters being simply abandoned.

One of the city's many Air Raid Prevention (ARP) positions was atop Jenners Department Store.

Because Edinburgh did not suffer a blitz, attitudes towards the air raids were often lax. Many people did not bother going down into the shelters, and often flouted the blackout. RAF pilots from Turnhouse once described Princes Street as being lit up at night like Wembley Stadium.

The blacked-out streets caused many accidents. Eventually, in the name of safety, it was decided to turn on the lights when a train was passing through the Commercial Street level crossing in Leith. Unfortunately this decision was not actually implemented, because none of the official bodies involved was willing to pay for the electricity.

If mass casualties had occurred, the dead would have been taken to one of the twenty-one church halls designated as mortuaries – or to the greyhound racing stadium at Stenhouse.

It was perhaps a good thing that the somewhat ramshackle air-raid assistance network was never called upon to deal with a major blitz. One of the most spectacular attacks of the war took place during the night of 29 September 1940, when a distillery warehouse on Duff Street, southwest of Haymarket Station, went up in a conflagration fuelled by a million gallons of whisky. On this occasion, as the blaze spread to neighbouring streets, the municipal command and control system was entirely unable to cope.

Experience from the Clydebank Blitz of April 1941 had shown that morale could be severely affected if the survivors of air raids could not get hold of tobacco. Edinburgh therefore stockpiled 50,000 cigarettes in case of emergencies.

Scrap metal drives saw the removal of garden railings throughout Edinburgh, with stocks piling up at a scrap yard in Leith Docks. Only when the war was over was it admitted that the wrought-iron railings were useless for recycling. The entire exercise had just been a bit of morale-boosting – 'everyone can do their bit'.

The best novels about Edinburgh during the war are *The Ferret Was Abraham's Daughter* (1949) and *Jezebel's Dust* (1951), both by Fred Urquhart, with vivid descriptions of the way the war changed the social, economic and sexual lives of two young women from the slums.

Edinburgh writer George Scott-Moncrieff recalled that the jubilation of VE Day in Edinburgh was muted because there was no obvious gathering place. Holyrood Palace was closed, the castle inaccessible, and the monolithic Scottish Office at St Andrews House was both unwelcoming and a symbol of English dominion. Lacking the focus of places such as George Square in Glasgow or London's Trafalgar Square, Edinburgh's revellers celebrated the end of the war by homing in on the American Red Cross in Princes Street, where the GIs distributed cigarettes and gum.

EVACUATION

The evacuation of children from the city did not go as the authorities anticipated. Of more than 64,000 children on the planning list, only 26,000 actually left, just over 40 per cent of the total. Once the expected saturation bombing did not take place, the evacuees started to drift back, and by March 1941 just 4,118 Edinburgh children were scattered across the more rural areas of Scotland.

Many schools were closed during the early months of the war, or were pressed into service as air-raid wardens' posts or first-aid centres. As a result, thousands of children were left to roam the streets, leading to a massive spike in juvenile crime.

Many rural or small-town households taking in evacuees from Edinburgh were horrified to discover the degree of poverty and disease amongst their inner-city guests. Head lice, scabies and other infectious skin conditions were not welcome visitors. Many small boys and girls had to undergo intense cleansing before settling in; while housewives up and down Scotland found themselves having to delouse the bedding their evacuees had slept in.

While some children were sent as far away as Inverness, many others ended up in two large school camps, one in Gorebridge (Midlothian) and the other at Broomlee near West Linton (Scottish Borders).

THE WAR OF DECEPTION

Deception was a key part of British strategy. 'Q' sites – decoy locations brightly-lit with fires at night – were set up at Turnhouse, Drem and Ratho, distracting the German bombers from genuine targets. Another 'Starfish Decoy', where controlled fires were set, was located at Cramond, close to a decoy anti-aircraft battery at Silverknowes, which featured wooden poles masquerading as genuine AA guns. A further decoy anti-aircraft battery was constructed off Millerhill Road on the east side of the city, with yet another Starfish fire decoy close to what is now the A720 by-pass.

In 1944, as the pace increased for an Allied invasion of Europe, Operation Fortitude North created an entirely fake invasion of Norway. Double agents assured their supposed masters in Germany that the British Fourth Army – an entirely imaginary force – was amassing in Edinburgh while an invasion fleet was being put together at Methil. Radio vans drove up and down the east coast, relaying signals from the fictional units. The deception worked, and large German forces continued to be maintained in Norway, preventing their deployment to France, where the real invasion of D-Day took place.

WAR WORK

Although Edinburgh had nowhere near the productive capacity of other Scottish industrial centres such as Glasgow, the city did manufacture key products for the war effort.

Ferranti made secret gyroscopic gunsights, and Fountainbridge Mill produced thousands of unglamorous but essential rubber items such as carburettor diaphragms and respirators. The Brunton wireworks at Musselburgh, with a workforce of 2,000, made catapults for aircraft carriers.

The industrial unrest that plagued inter-war Britain did not cease just because there was a war on. In April 1940, eighty workers at Niddrie Brickworks downed tools, and 300 men went on strike at Henry Robb's shipyard in Leith.

Despite the strike, Henry Robb's record during the war was impressive. The shipyard built forty-two navy and fourteen merchant vessels, plus repaired some 3,000 ships. This output included corvettes, frigates, mine-sweepers, and pipelayers for PLUTO, the underwater pipeline that supplied oil for the Allied armies invading Europe.

From late 1943 Henry Robb also manufactured major parts of one of the Mulberry Harbours, the floating docks that enabled the Allied forces to land men and equipment on D-Day without having to take one of the French ports. A new construction yard was built on land reclaimed from the Forth, and 600 men and women laboured to build thirteen pier-heads and sixteen large pontoons to an extraordinarily tight timescale – one pier-head every week. Of course, at the time the project was top secret and none of the workers at Leith knew exactly why what they were building was so important.

As soon as each 'Hippo' pier-head was completed it was towed to Newhaven. The components were then towed *en masse* to the south coast of England by ocean-going tugs built at Leith. On 6 June 1944 the same tugs helped take the parts of the Mulberry Harbours across to Normandy and the Allied invasion of Nazi-occupied Europe.

5

CRIME AND PUNISHMENT

THE MAJESTY OF THE LAW

Lord Braxfield, the most prominent judge of the Justiciary Court in the 1780s, was notorious as a hard-drinking gambler who swore like a trooper. He once sent two advocates home because they were hung-over in court, one reeking of punch and the other 'belching claret' (and his Lordship would definitely have been able to make the distinction). A story was told that, when convicting murderer Matthew Hay – an old friend against whom he had often played chess – Braxfield exclaimed, 'That's checkmate now, Matty!' Sadly for the supposed truth of this otherwise excellent tale, Braxfield could not play chess, and the anecdote belongs to an anonymous judge.

Andrew Crosbie was a noted New Town lawyer, and probably provided the model for the character of Paulus Pleydell in Sir Walter Scott's *Guy Mannering*. One day Crosbie was pleading a case on behalf of a farmer, but his heart was not in it. Whenever he started coming to a lacklustre close, however, his client slipped a coin wrapped in white paper into the lawyer's pocket. Assuming the coins were guineas (worth £1 1s each), Mr Crosbie rediscovered his eloquence, and by the time fourteen coins were nestling in his pocket, he had won the case. Only when the triumphant lawyer attempted to buy a celebratory bottle of wine did he unwrap the coins – to discover he had been paid not in guineas, but in farthings.

In 1609 King James VI brought Sir Robert Logan of Restalrig to the dock for treason. Which was strange, seeing as Sir Robert had already been dead for three years. Nevertheless, the bones of the corpse were displayed in court, and found guilty of taking part in the Gowrie Conspiracy, an attempt to abduct or murder the king in 1600. The Logan family – notorious as a volatile, piratical and extortionist gang in the Leith area – were stripped of their noble status and had their wealth and property forfeited.

HANGED BY THE NECK UNTIL YE BE DEAD

In the 1590s a bailiff confiscated the goods of a debtor and, as was usual, exposed them for auction at the Mercat Cross, the place of public execution. Many of the items for sale were attached to the gibbet itself, including a painting of James VI and Queen Anne. King James was not amused at this insult and had the bailiff hanged – from the same gallows, naturally.

As well as the Mercat Cross on the Royal Mile, places of execution included the Grassmarket, and the Blew Stane, a boulder on Castle Hill which is now covered by the Castle Esplanade.

Another site was the Borough Muir south of the city, which was often pressed into use when there was a queue at the other gallows. Between 23 April 1603 and 14 July 1604, for example, twenty-one members of the outlawed Clan MacGregor were hanged at the Cross, five were hanged and one beheaded on Castle Hill, and eleven hanged on the Borough Muir, the latter used because, when the list of ordinary malefactors was taken into account, the main gallows in the city centre were simply too busy.

Sometimes gallows were set up at the scene of the crime. On 25 January 1815 Thomas Kelly and Henry O'Neill were hanged at the junction of Braid Road and Comiston Road, the very spot where they had committed highway robbery. The stone bases for the gibbets can still be seen on Braid Road.

In 1821 an unusual autobiography appeared: *The Life of David Haggart, alias John Wilson, alias John Morison, alias Barney McCoul, alias John McColgan, alias Daniel O'Brien, alias The Switcher*. According to the title page, it was 'written by himself, while under sentence of death.' The book is a treasure trove of criminal slang: 'snibs' (pickpockets), 'geaches' (thieves), 'blones' (girls), 'bulkies' (the police), 'hoys' (shoplifting) 'wedge' and 'dross' (silver and gold), 'screaves' (banknotes) and, my favourite, 'yelpers' (wild animals). Edinburgh-born Haggart was a successful career thief, only twenty years old at the time of his execution. He had escaped from prison four times, but during the last break-out, in Dumfries, had killed the guard. Haggart dictated his autobiography to his lawyer from the condemned cell in Edinburgh Jail.

Where a crime did not warrant the death penalty, the authorities had recourse to a range of barbaric punishments, including piercing the tongue with a red-hot spike, 'clipping' the lower part of the ear, or branding the cheek. The last public whipping in Edinburgh took place as late as 1822.

PRISONS

Because Canongate was a separate burgh from Edinburgh, it was entitled to its own jail or tolbooth. The present Canongate Tolbooth was built in 1591 on the site of a previous jail. In its later years the tolbooth was the uncomfortable home for a number of civil debtors, some of whom consoled themselves by 'fishing' in Tolbooth Wynd at the rear of the prison. A string would be thrown down, to which the debtor's friends would attach a bottle of Lochrin or Sunbury whisky, and the happy prisoner would haul up his 'catch'.

The Edinburgh Tolbooth, made famous by Sir Walter Scott in his novel *The Heart of Midlothian*, is now only remembered by the heart-shaped stonework in the pavement of the High Street. Vile, stinking and cramped, the prison was hated so much that it became customary to spit on the heart, something that visitors are still encouraged to do.

The base of the Mercat Cross holds a tiny Victorian cell for the temporary imprisonment of malefactors apprehended on the Royal Mile.

Several Bridewells and Houses of Correction rose and fell during the seventeenth and eighteenth centuries, all of which are now lost. From 1817 to 1925 the western side of Calton Hill was dominated by the mass of Calton Jail, designed to hold more serious offenders than those typically incarcerated in the Bridewells. The prison site is now the offices of St Andrew's House – ten murderers, executed at the jail, are buried beneath the car park.

Saughton Prison was colloquially known as the Big Hotel.

THE POLICE – THE EARLY DAYS

From the early seventeenth century Edinburgh had part-time officials called Constables, who were effectively an arm of the Town Council, and provided what we would only barely recognise as policing.

The first body that might vaguely be called a police force was the Standing Watch or City Guard, a body of sixty soldiers under the command of a captain. Formed in 1648, their duty was to keep order rather than to prevent or investigate crime. After a few years the Town Council got fed up with paying for the guard, and substituted a semi-voluntary requirement for male citizens to serve on a rota basis. This cost-cutting exercise was a disaster, and the City Guard was reinstituted in 1679.

The City Guard was not exactly the last word in probity. The men were sometimes lethally over-zealous with their weaponry, and often took bribes; and in 1679 their commander was dismissed after being convicted of counterfeiting coins. The last Captain of the Guard, James Burnet, was a habitual drunk and weighed 19 stone, much of which was accounted for by his prodigious beer belly; it is hard to imagine this fat controller chasing after a villain round the streets of Edinburgh.

In the eighteenth century the Old Town was perhaps more effectively policed by the Society of Cadies, a group of street-wise lads-for-hire who operated as impromptu messengers, bodyguards, valets, procurers and agents for any service that residents or visitors might desire. In 1775 Captain Edward Topham, visiting from England, noted that the Cadies, knowing where the criminals lived and stashed their loot, also operated as 'thief-takers'. 'It is entirely owing to them that there are fewer robberies and less housebreaking in Edinburgh than anywhere else,' wrote Topham, who sounded like a satisfied customer.

The word 'cadies' continues in use as the caddies of the golf course.

The much-hated City Guard was disbanded in 1817. The Constables, meanwhile, now called the High Constables and largely composed of well-heeled gentlemen, became more of a ceremonial institution. Both organisations were replaced by something new in the city: a professional, full-time, uniformed police force.

The Edinburgh Police was founded in 1805. The senior officer in the city was known as the Superintendent of Police, who also sat as a judge on low-level crimes in the new Police Court. The command structure devolved through Inspectors, Sergeants, Constables and Watchmen.

The very first Police Inspectors were hardly seasoned criminalists, as, apart from a former Captain of the City Guard, they included a baker, a grocer, a painter, a merchant and a bookseller. However, all new police forces need to start somewhere, and within a short time the Inspectors were operating long shifts out of watchhouses in the High Street, George Street, Teviot Row and Portobello.

A number of police officers of different ranks were discharged from the force in the early years, often on a charge of 'dereliction of duty', usually a code phrase for drunkenness.

From the start, the police were distinguished from the quasi-military City Guard by the fact that the coppers were not armed (other than with a wooden baton). The muskets and bayonets of the despised City Guard had been over-used over the years, and the new police force was conceived of as maintaining order by consent, rather than by force of arms.

The idea of the 'detective' as a police rank took a while to gel. Between 1808 and 1813 James Denovan was the Intendant of Police at Leith, effectively acting as a detective by making enquiries into the background and movements of suspected criminals. In 1819 Edinburgh created a new police rank of Captain-Lieutenant, specifically responsible for making criminal enquiries. Soon, plain-clothes 'Criminal Officers' (the early version of CID) were making their way up through the ranks.

Irishman James McLevy joined the Edinburgh Police Force in 1830. Probably the most successful detective of his day, he claimed to have personally solved no fewer than 2,220 cases. In 1861

he wrote his memoirs, a racy account filled with 'nightingales' (streetwalkers), 'bullies' (pimps), pickpockets, muggers and various other ne'er-do-wells.

In McLevy's time many of the Old Town 'lands' had degenerated into thieves' rookeries, two of which – Happy Land and Holy Land, on the now-vanished Leith Wynd at the west end of Canongate – were also the most notorious and dangerous brothels in the city. In 1840 there were 203 brothels in Edinburgh, of which only three were classified as 'clean and decent'. Most of the nightingales and bullies operated out of noisome taverns, cheap eating-houses, and even the public stairwells of the lands themselves.

THE POLICE IN THE 20TH CENTURY

More than 500 police officers from Edinburgh and the surrounding forces enlisted to fight in what was known as the Great War. At least seventy-eight were killed, around 15 per cent of the total.

Fewer officers joined up in the Second World War because the police was a reserved occupation, needed for the home front.

On 18 July 1940 Assistant Chief Constable Robert Thomson, on his way to a call out during an air-raid blackout, was shot at a checkpoint in Milton Road West by RAF Sergeant Alexander McPherson, who was drunk. McPherson was convicted of culpable homicide, but only served six months in prison after the jury made a plea for leniency.

In October 1940 a man acting suspiciously was arrested by the police at Waverley Station. According to his fake Swiss passport he was Werner Walti, but a suitcase filled with German maps of Britain, a wireless, codes and a Mauser automatic pistol showed otherwise. He had landed on the Banffshire coast with two other agents of the Abwehr, the German Secret Service. On 6 August 1941 Robert Petter – his real name – was hanged as a spy at Wandsworth Jail. Detective Superintendent William Merrielees, who made the arrest disguised as a station porter, went on to become the Chief Constable of Lothian and Peebles from 1950 to 1968.

THE POLICE TODAY

In 2010/11 Edinburgh had less crime per head of population than Glasgow, Aberdeen and Dundee.

In 2012, twenty-two of the city's police boxes were put up for sale. Each of the distinctive large rectangles, which were installed in the early 1930s with inbuilt telephones, weighed 2 tonnes. Almost all of those purchased have been converted into coffee kiosks, shops, bureaux de change, and similar establishments. A condition of the sale was that the new owners had to paint over the original blue colour, to make it clear they were no longer 'police'.

Another twenty boxes remained within police ownership, and as part of a community engagement initiative, three – on Duddingston Road West, Jocks Lodge and Craigentinny Road, all in the southeast of the city – were re-opened in 2012 for the first time in decades.

Edinburgh City Police and Leith Police merged after the respective councils joined in 1920. In 1975 the Edinburgh Police vanished, merging with the Lothians and Peebles Constabulary and the Berwick, Roxburgh and Selkirk Constabulary to form Lothian and Borders Police, with an HQ in Fettes Avenue.

In 2013 Lothian and Borders Police, along with the other seven Scottish forces, was incorporated into a new national police force, the Police Service of Scotland.

EARLY CCTV?

As a boy, George Scott-Moncrieff frequently visited the Camera Obscura in the Outlook Tower, always hoping to see a dastardly crime underway on a nearby roof-top, the perpetrator entirely unaware that he was being secretly watched from the pinhole camera in the tourist attraction. Sadly, the future Edinburgh writer and historian never got his wish.

6

CITY OF CULTURE

LITERATURE

In 2004 Edinburgh was declared the first UNESCO City of Literature, recognising the city's role as a world centre for literature and literary activity.

Edinburgh is intimately connected with such literary legends as Sir Walter Scott, Robert Louis Stevenson, Robert Burns, Sir Arthur Conan Doyle, Ian Rankin and J.K. Rowling, and their lives and works, along with those of many other writers, are celebrated throughout the city with statues, memorials, plaques, placenames and tours. You can't go far in Edinburgh without realising the scale of the city's literary heritage.

Other UNESCO Cities of Literature that have followed in Edinburgh's wake are Melbourne, Iowa City, Dublin, Reykjavik and Norwich.

In the early 1960s Edinburgh had the highest ratio of book sales to population in the entire world.

In 2011 the Edinburgh International Book Festival recorded 303,541 attendees, although of course many of those would have gone to more than one event.

10 NOVELS ABOUT EDINBURGH THAT YOU MUST READ

1. *The Expedition of Humphry Clinker* by Tobias Smollett (1771). Still funny after all these years.

2. *The Private Memoirs of a Justified Sinner* by James Hogg (1824). Still scary after all these years.

3. *Catriona* by Robert Louis Stevenson (1893). The follow-up to *Kidnapped*.

4. *The Prime of Miss Jean Brodie* by Muriel Spark (1961). Pre-war schooldays and philosophy, writ large.

5. *Trainspotting* by Irvine Welsh (1993). Junkies, sick jokes and the most disgusting toilet in Scotland.

6. *Complicity* by Iain Banks (1993). A serial killer is offing the rich and wicked.

7. *Quite Ugly One Morning* by Christopher Brookmyre (1996). Tartan noir. Nasty.

8. *The Fanatic* by James Robertson (2000). Good vs. Evil; 1997 Edinburgh vs. the 1677 version.

9. *44 Scotland Street* by Alexander McCall Smith (2005). Full of Edinburgh jokes; Ian Rankin turns up as a character.

10. *The Last Watch* by Sergei Lukyanenko (2008). There's a real vampire loose in the Edinburgh Dungeon horror show attraction.

10 NOVELS BY EDINBURGH WRITERS THAT YOU MUST READ

1. *Coral Island* by R.M. Ballantyne (1857). Classic children's adventure.

2. *Treasure Island* by Robert Louis Stevenson (1883). Long John Silver, Blind Pew, pirates....

3. *The Wind in the Willows* by Kenneth Grahame (1908). Meet Mole, Ratty, Badger and the irrepressible Mr Toad.

4. *A Study in Scarlet* (1887) by Sir Arthur Conan Doyle. Sherlock Holmes' first appearance.

5. *The Lost World* (1912) by Sir Arthur Conan Doyle. Dinosaurs in the South American jungle.

6. *Harry Potter and the Philosopher's Stone* by J.K. Rowling (1997). The boy wizard's first outing.

7. *The No. 1 Ladies' Detective Agency* by Alexander McCall Smith (1998). Botswana's best detective agency. Utterly beguiling.

8. *Maps of Hell* by Paul Johnston (2010). Murder and madness in Maine.

9. & 10. *The Journal of a Tour to the Hebrides* (1785) and *The Life of Samuel Johnson* (1791) by James Boswell – OK, these aren't novels, but literature would be all the poorer without the waspish, witty and indiscreet 'Boswellian' biographical style pioneered by this Edinburgh writer.

EDINBURGH'S TOP TEN FICTIONAL DETECTIVES

1. Sir Arthur Conan Doyle never brought Sherlock Holmes to Edinburgh, but Caleb Carr does that in his 2005 Holmes and Watson pastiche *The Italian Secretary*, wherein a number of well-known elements of Holyrood Palace, from Mary, Queen of Scots to the murder of her Italian secretary David Rizzio, are worked into a dastardly plot of greed and murder.

2. It's 1828 and Edinburgh is up to its oxters in bodysnatchers. But Napoleonic War veteran Sergeant Adam Quire of the Edinburgh City Police is more concerned with a series of gruesome murders committed by something that seems not quite human... Brian Ruckley's *The Edinburgh Dead* (2010) atmospherically uses Edinburgh locations and real historical characters to evoke a sense of urban dread.

3. It's 2020 and Britain has collapsed into tribal chaos. Edinburgh, however, is ruled by a hardline quasi-Communist intellectual elite, who run the Festival 365 days a year. But when it comes to solving murders, the totalitarian establishment has to turn to private investigator Quintilian 'Quint' Dalrymple, whose unsavoury personal habits include listening to banned music such as the blues. Paul Johnston's future-crime novels *Body Politic*, *The Bone Yard*, *Water of Death*, *The Blood Tree* and *The House of Dust* (1997-2002) re-imagine well-known Edinburgh locations and preoccupations in a satirical dystopic light.

4. Since his first appearance in *Enter Second Murderer* (1988), Inspector Faro of the Edinburgh City Police has been dealing with the full range of Victorian criminals, from aristocratic poisoners to enemies of the British Empire, in a dozen novels by the prolific Alanna Knight.

5. Detective Sergeant Alice Rice has investigated four novels' worth of crimes since *Blood in the Water* (2007), all informed by author Gillian Galbraith's in-depth knowledge of legal and medical procedures, drawn from her previous career as an advocate practising at the Scottish Bar.

6. Jackson Brodie is a former copper turned private investigator with a complicated private life; his visit to the Edinburgh Fringe in Kate Atkinson's *One Good Turn* (2006) makes his life even more complicated. Brodie returns to Edinburgh in the brilliantly intricate *When Will There Be Good News?* (2008), and the books were adapted for television in 2011 as *Case Histories*.

7. In twenty-two books since *Skinner's Rules* in 1993, Quentin Jardine's hard-headed establishment cop Bob Skinner has

moved from Detective Chief Superintendent to Chief Constable, no less, but he's still got time to solve crimes, bloody, brutal and baffling. In an off-shoot novel, *The Loner* (2011), Jardine dedicates the book to Robert Gordon Skinner QPM (Queen's Police Medal), maintaining the novel's contention that Skinner is a real person in the real world, and, as a friend of Jardine, helped get the book written.

8. Detective Inspector Rob Brennan is a troubled soul, and his troubles get worse with every brutal killing. Tony Black's police procedurals *Truth Lies Bleeding* (2011) and *Murder Mile* (2012) explore the dark heart of contemporary Edinburgh.

9. Isabel Dalhousie is well off, a philosopher concerned with moral dilemmas, and something of an amateur sleuth. Read Alexander McCall Smith's *The Sunday Philosophy Club* (2004), fall in love with the character, and devour the rest of the series.

10. When it comes to Edinburgh detectives, however, the daddy is Detective Inspector John Rebus. First appearing in *Knots and Crosses* in 1987, Ian Rankin's grumpy, introspective rock music fan has racked up eighteen hugely popular crime novels and numerous short stories, the most recent being *Standing in Another Man's Grave* (2012). Rebus – whose name means 'puzzle' – has acted both as a disquisition on the nature of Scottish masculinity, and, at times, on the 'state of the nation' of Scotland itself. Edinburgh is a central character in most of the novels – if Sir Walter Scott defined the place of Edinburgh in the popular imagination for the nineteenth century, Ian Rankin has achieved the same status in our times.

STREET NAMES WITH LITERARY CONNECTIONS

Sir Walter Scott was one of the most popular authors of the nineteenth century, and his fictions have often been mistaken for genuine Scottish history. Along the way, he invented many of the country's present 'traditions', including the widespread wearing of tartan and the kilt. He is also the most celebrated writer to be found in Edinburgh street names. As well as having an Avenue named after him in Liberton, Scott's characters, places and book titles appear in:

Redgauntlet Terrace, Fairford Grove and Summertrees Court *(Redgauntlet)*
Mannering Place, Dinmont Drive, Hazelwood Grove and Ellangowan Terrace *(Guy Mannering)*
Lammermoor Terrace, Ashton Grove, Balderston Gardens and Ravenswood Avenue *(The Bride of Lammermoor)*
Marmion Crescent *(Marmion)*
Durward Grove *(Quentin Durward)*
Saddletree Loan *(The Heart of Midlothian)*
Dundrennan Cottages and Glendinning Crescent *(The Abbott)*
Claverhouse Drive, Headrigg Row and Bellenden Gardens *(Old Mortality)*
Woodstock Place *(Woodstock)*
Talisman Place *(The Talisman)*
Kenilworth Drive, Tressilian Grove and Cumnor Crescent *(Kenilworth)*
Glenvarloch Crescent, Ringwood Place and Nigel Loan *(The Fortunes of Nigel)*
Monksbarns Gardens, Glenallan Drive and Ochiltree Gardens *(The Antiquary)*
Ivanhoe Crescent *(Ivanhoe)*
Peveril Terrace *(Peveril of the Peak)*
Hazeldean Terrace *(Jock o'Hazeldean)*

In the same area of Liberton we also have Rutherford Drive, Anne Rutherford being Scott's mother.

Alan Breck, one of the central characters in Robert Louis Stevenson's *Kidnapped*, is commemorated by Alan Breck Gardens in South Clermiston. Other names in the neighbourhood taken from the same novel are Dochart Drive, Duart Crescent, Durar Drive, Essendean Place, Glenure Loan, Hoseason Gardens, Morven Street, Rannoch Grove and Torrance Park. In the novel, David Balfour, the novel's narrator, crosses Clermiston Hill before looking down on the dread House of Shaws in Cramond.

Robert Burns has a Drive next to an Avenue named for his wife Jean Armour. Nearby is Clarinda Terrace, 'Clarinda' being Agnes

Craig McLehose, the subject of Burns' unrequited ardour and the muse for his most famous love poem. 'Ae Fond Kiss'. In the same development at Kirk Brae are Alloway Loan, named for Burns' birthplace; Mossgiel Walk, commemorating the farm where Burns' famous poem 'To a Mouse' was composed; and Shanter Way, a direct reference to 'Tam O' Shanter'.

Rankin Drive, Avenue and Road in West Mains are named after the seventeenth-century William Rankine, not contemporary crime novelist Ian Rankin. However, the only person in the Edinburgh phone book who shares a surname with Rankin's iconic detective Rebus lives on – Rankin Drive.

WRITERS' LIVES

James Tytler (1747-1805) edited and wrote most of the second edition of the *Encyclopaedia Britannica*, which made a profit of £45,000 for the publishers. Tytler was paid 12 guineas (£12 12s).

The poet W.E. Henley, who had had his left leg amputated below the knee, was the inspiration for the character Long John Silver in *Treasure Island*, the novel written by Henley's friend Robert Louis Stevenson.

The beauteous Stella Cartwright was the muse for the many 1950s intellectuals who congregated around the pubs of Rose Street – probably half the writers in the city were in love with her at one point. Every year on her birthday Orkney poet George Mackay Brown sent Cartwright an acrostic poem, where the first letter of each line spelled out a personal message. Cartwright descended into alcoholism and died, alone, in 1985.

In 1822 the English literary critic and essayist William Hazlitt spent four days in Edinburgh, where, under the more liberal laws north of the border, he was able to obtain a divorce that would allow him to marry again. When he returned to London, however, Hazlitt discovered that his intended bride was seeing someone else.

In August 1811 a hot-headed poet named William Bysshe Shelley, nineteen years old, arrived in Edinburgh on the mail coach with Harriet Westbrook, just sixteen. They had eloped and were underage in England. Neither met the residence or legal requirements in Edinburgh either, but false documentation soon saw them getting married at the Leith Wynd Chapel of Ease on the Canongate. Seven years later the minister who performed the ceremony was defrocked for making a habit of such illegal weddings.

Charles Kirkpatrick Sharpe (1781-1851) was an eccentric antiquarian who collected ballads, erotica and folk music, and wrote books on everything from witchcraft to aristocratic scandals and bizarre family histories. Acid-tongued, he once said of Sir Walter Scott, 'he spouts without mercy' and described Shelley as living on nothing but 'arsenic, aquafortis [nitric acid in water] and half-an-hour's sleep in the night.' After Sharpe's death the auction of his extraordinary library took eight days, while another six days were required to sell his collection of curiosities, which included a mummified cat, a murderer's hand, a cap worn by Mary Queen of Scots, various human bones, a stuffed crocodile, and a 'Feejee Mermaid' – a fake mermaid constructed from a fish and a monkey.

When James Boswell boasted to his guest Samuel Johnson that the view of the Firth of Forth from Castle Hill was 'the finest prospect in Europe,' the famous curmudgeon shrugged and answered, 'Ay, that is the state of the world. Water is the same everywhere.'

In August 1917 Siegfried Sassoon and Wilfred Owen, two of the country's greatest war poets, met for the first time, the venue being the Craiglockhart War Hospital for Nervous Disorders. The meeting inspired Pat Barker's *Regeneration* trilogy.

Father John Gray of St Peter's Church in Morningside had, in his earlier life in London, been an acolyte and lover of Oscar Wilde. He was probably the major inspiration for the central character in Wilde's 1890 novel *The Picture of Dorian Gray*, in which a dissolute young man remains beautiful while his portrait decays with corruption and age. Gray later entered the priesthood and very likely moved to Edinburgh to be as far away from the dangerously scandal-prone Wilde as possible. In an entirely unrelated episode, Oscar Wilde lectured at Edinburgh's Queen Street Hall on 20 December 1884. His talks, on 'Dress' and 'The Value of Art in Modern Life' attracted, according to *The Scotsman*, 'a meagre attendance.' Wilde said of Edinburgh: 'It is quite lovely,' then adding, 'some of it.'

According to his biographer John Rae, Adam Smith, the author of the world-changing work on economics, *The Wealth of Nations*, began life by being stolen by gypsies.

GRAPHIC NOVELS AND COMICS

The Dogs of Edinburgh (2012) is a graphic novel spin-off of the popular American paranormal TV series *Supernatural*. Spook-hunter Sam Winchester teams up with the toothsome Emma of the Isles to fight supernatural beasties in Edinburgh.

Batman came to Edinburgh in 1998. *Batman: Scottish Connection* by Alan Grant and Frank Quitely has Bruce Wayne attending a family reunion in Scotland, which includes a boat trip under the Forth Bridge and a visit to the supposed mysteries of the Knights Templar at Rosslyn Chapel, wherein everything turns a tad Dan 'The Da Vinci Code' Brown. You get to see Bruce Wayne in a kilt, but sadly not Batman – for that pleasure, you have to turn to 'The Lord of Batmanor', an episode in *Detective Comics #198* from 1953, although Edinburgh doesn't feature in the story.

In 2007 Alan Grant adapted Robert Louis Stevenson's *Kidnapped* – part of which takes place in Edinburgh – into a graphic novel, with a Scots language version, *Kidnappit*, also being published. The following year Grant produced a graphic novel version of the definitive work of Edinburgh Gothic, Stevenson's *The Strange Case of Dr. Jekyll and Mr. Hyde.*

LIBRARIES

Edinburgh had the first lending library in Britain. Opened by poet, wigmaker and bookseller Allan Ramsay in 1728, it operated out of a 'Luckenbooth' stall beside St Giles Cathedral, and grew to hold an astonishing 30,000 volumes. The Revd Robert Wodrow, a Presbyterian sourpuss, described it as a place where, 'All the villainous, profane and obscene books and plays, as printed in London' were available, at a cheap price, to 'young boys and servant women.' Young people and women reading books: shocking.

Edinburgh is a world centre for libraries and archives. Among the key institutions are:

The National Library of Scotland on George IV Bridge, one of the only six legal deposit libraries in the UK, meaning it is entitled to a copy of every printed item published. The reference library – which is open to anyone – is the biggest library in Scotland and holds the largest collection of Scottish-related material in the world. The NLS has more than 15 million books and other printed items. To maximize storage space, the books in the stacks are not stored upright by catalogue number – but horizontally, by size.

The Advocates Library in Parliament House, a private law library owned by the Faculty of Advocates. Founded in 1689 with a remit much greater than merely dealing with legal books, by the Victorian era it was effectively the principal historical and reference library for the Scottish nation. In 1925 the Advocates Library gifted 750,000 volumes to the new National Library of Scotland, and the legal collection can be accessed via the NLS catalogue.

The Signet Library on Parliament Square, a restricted law library that, however, is often hired out for weddings and corporate events on account of its magnificent interior.

The National Records of Scotland (formerly the National Archives of Scotland) in Register House at the east end of Princes Street is the nation's primary depository of legal, financial and personal documents. It is an essential resource for anyone researching their family history.

As well as these individual institutions, Edinburgh has a network of twenty-eight public libraries, plus specialist sections dedicated to art, children's books, and music. The Edinburgh and Scottish Collection in the basement of the Central Library on George IV Bridge is the premier destination for anyone researching the history of the city.

Since 2009 the Central Library lending department has had an unusual permanent resident – an inflatable Dalek. *Dr Who*'s most persistent enemy has been periodically used to illustrate various books and films, including *Dalek Potter and the Chamber of Secrets*, *Saving*

Private Dalek, *The Dalek with the Dragon Tattoo* and *The Good, the Bad and the Dalek*. For *Count Dalek* the inflatable was hung upside down like a vampire bat.

A cardboard Cyberman also makes regular appearances in the library.

The same library is decorated with a set of beautiful nineteenth-century tiles manufactured by Burmantofts in Leeds. Installed in 1890 as a continuous frieze around the basement newsroom (now the Edinburgh and Scottish Library Room), the tiles are now in a stairwell, and via individual letters spell out apt quotations from the Book of Proverbs, chapter 8:
   'The fear of the Lord is the beginning of wisdom and the knowledge of the Holy is understanding.'
   'Take fast hold of Instruction let her not go keep her for she is thy life.'
   'Wisdom is the principal therefore get wisdom and with all thy getting get understanding.'

NEWSPAPERS

Edinburgh's first newspaper was the *Edinburgh Courant*, which launched in February 1705, price one penny. It came out twice a week for five years, before changing its name to the *Scots Courant*, while in 1718 the *Edinburgh Evening Courant* appeared, reverting to the *Edinburgh Courant* name again in 1871. All of which establishes the confusing tendency of newspapers to change names, merge, disappear, reappear under different names and ownership, and generally make any idea of a smooth, sensible history impossible.

The *Edinburgh Advertiser* started up in 1764. It merged with its main competitor, the *Edinburgh Evening Courant*, in 1859. The *Caledonian Mercury* had a longer run, from 1720 to 1867. The *Edinburgh Evening Dispatch*, first published in 1886, merged with its rival the *Edinburgh Evening News* in 1963, the resulting *Edinburgh Evening News and Dispatch* finally becoming the *Evening News* in 1967. The *Evening News* is now one of the only two daily newspapers published in Edinburgh. The other, *The Scotsman*, first appeared as a weekly publication in 1817.

In 1855 *The Scotsman* became the first daily newspaper in Scotland.

Traditionally, a rivalry existed between *The Scotsman* and the *Glasgow Herald*. This could be expressed in the subtlest of ways – for example, the Edinburgh paper always referred to itself as *The Scotsman*, while its Glaswegian rival delighted in dropping the initial capital T, hence 'the *Scotsman*'.

The *Edinburgh Gazette* is not an ordinary newspaper, being a twice-weekly official paper of the British Government. As the publication of record, it is the place to go if you are looking for notices relating to matters of state or governance, public finances, the awarding of medals and state honours, and notices of bankruptcy or insolvency. First published in 1699, the *Edinburgh Gazette* has been printed continuously since 1793.

THEATRES

Edinburgh today is synonymous with theatre and performance, as the Festival, the Fringe, and the vibrant year-round cultural scene testify. It may be surprising to learn, then, that plays were once banned in the city.

Edinburgh's very first theatre opened in Carrubber's Close off the High Street in 1736, under the management of the famous writer Allan Ramsay. The following year the establishment fell foul of the new Licensing Act, which forbade the performance of plays outside the City of London.

A little less than a decade later, the Canongate Theatre or Playhouse Theatre opened in Playhouse Close and managed to survive official and religious disapproval. The Canongate was eventually killed off by competition from the first Theatre Royal, which opened at the New Town end of North Bridge in 1767.

The Theatre Royal was itself rescued from financial oblivion in 1819 by the huge success of the operatic version of Sir Walter Scott's *Rob Roy*. The opera was still being performed a century later, with audiences booing and hissing the villain as if they were in a panto.

In 1756 a tragedy called *Douglas* was a huge success at the Playhouse (prompting an audience member on the first night to cry out, 'Whaur's yer Willie Shakespeare noo?'). Things didn't go quite so well for the playwright John Home however, as he happened to be a Church of Scotland minister, and the Presbyterian church took the view that plays were the tool of the Devil himself. Home was forced to resign from his parish.

PHOTOGRAPHY

From 1843 to 1848 David Octavius Hill and Robert Adamson occupied Rock House on Calton Hill, where they instituted an artistic revolution using the new medium of capturing light on photographic plates. Their series 'The Fishermen and Women of the Firth of Forth' may mark the beginning of photography as a medium of documenting a way of life. Both photography as a tool of anthropology, and the techniques of the observational television documentary, have their origins here.

ART

A new form of art was invented in Edinburgh in 1787. In that year portrait painter Robert Barker patented the Panorama, a 360-degree painting that surrounded the viewer. Barker's first Panorama was 'The View of Edinburgh' from the top of Calton Hill.

Lord Eldin, who lived at 16 Picardy Place, was a noted art collector. The auction after his death attracted so many people that the floor gave way. Around 100 people fell into the room below, some being seriously injured, and Mr Smith, a banker from Moray Place, died.

MOVIELAND EDINBURGH

A silent film version of Sir Walter Scott's classic Edinburgh novel *The Heart of Midlothian* was made in Hollywood in 1914, while *The Bride of Lammermoor* was filmed as early as 1908.

Waverley Steps (1947) is a semi-documentary film about a day in the life of Edinburgh, with the main roles played by local amateur actors. As a period piece it is quite beguiling, especially when highlighting the differences between the rich and the poor. The sights of the city are seen through the eyes of a visiting Danish seaman. In the original script the sailor, on docking, was supposed to have an assignation with a young lady of negotiable affection, but the Town Council wasn't going to tolerate a suggestion that Edinburgh (or more particularly, Leith) was a provider of those kinds of services. Watch out for a shot that got past the censors – as the camera moves past the elegant shoppers on Princes Street, a small boy is seen urinating into the gutter.

Happy Go Lovely (1950) is a piece of froth about a millionaire and a chorus girl cavorting to a backdrop of the Edinburgh Festival. It's entirely avoidable, even if it has David Niven in it.

Peter Sellers is an accountant with murder on his mind in the 1959 Hollywood comedy *The Battle of the Sexes*. An American efficiency expert comes to Edinburgh and clashes with Scottish attitudes to business. With numerous exterior shots, Edinburgh does a fine job of being itself, homicidal number-crunchers notwithstanding. Sellers is superb.

There's a great scene at the start of *Journey to the Centre of the Earth* (1959) where an absent-minded professor played by James Mason blithely meanders through a marching pipe band while reading a newspaper. The scene was filmed on the Mound, while the university's Old Quad was also pressed into service for the film's closing sequence.

Donaldson's School for the Deaf on Henderson Row (now part of Edinburgh Academy) was used as the Marcia Blane School for Girls in the film of *The Prime of Miss Jean Brodie* (1969). The exterior scenes were shot in locations such as Greyfriars churchyard and around the Grassmarket. Maggie Smith won an Oscar for her portrayal of the title character. If there's one Edinburgh film you should see, this is it.

Parts of *Chariots of Fire* (1981), the story of Olympic athletes Eric Liddell and Harold Abrahams, were filmed in the Old Town,

Holyrood Park and in the stadiums at Inverleith and Goldenacre, as well as within the elegant confines of the Café Royal, just off the east end of Princes Street.

Scottish comedy *Restless Natives* (1985) interleaves its Highland scenery with scenes in Newhaven, Wester Hailes, Holyrood Park, The Mound and the Old Town.

1989's *The Conquest of the South Pole* combined grim housing schemes and the grandeur of Arthur's Seat to tell the story of a group of unemployed youths attempting to recreate a polar journey in Edinburgh.

Blue Black Permanent (1992), a drama spanning several decades in the twentieth century, used a number of Old Town locations to good effect.

The contemporary film noir *Shallow Grave* (1994) was set in the New Town, but apart from a few exteriors, most of the movie was shot in a warehouse in Glasgow.

Tickets to the Zoo (1994) focused on Edinburgh's young homeless and unemployed, to rather less effect than the game-changing, epochal *Trainspotting* (1996), a cheery coal-black comedy about heroin addicts. Although the iconic 'Choose life...' opening chase scene in *Trainspotting* was filmed in Edinburgh, many of the film's interiors were shot in Glasgow. One scene, where the central characters attack and rob an American visitor in an Edinburgh pub, gave the Scottish tourist board the heebie-jeebies.

Hold Back the Night (1999) starts with the main characters scoring drugs in the Grassmarket before fleeing north.

Complicity (2000), the dark movie of Iain Banks' dark novel of the same name, liberally uses locations in Edinburgh, South Queensferry and the Forth.

Some of the scenes in the troubling thriller *Young Adam* (2003) were filmed on the Union Canal around Edinburgh.

REEL LIFE

What may have been the first example of moving pictures being presented to a paying audience in Scotland took place at the Empire Palace Theatre on 13 April 1896. Unfortunately technical problems meant that the brand-new medium of the 'Cinematographe' rather underperformed on the night.

The silent newsreels *Theatre Fire in Edinburgh* and *Funeral of the Great Lafayette* (both 1911) show the aftermath of a fire at the Empire Palace in which ten people died, including Lafayette, an escapologist and illusionist in the same league as Houdini. Lafayette's lion, the disappearance of which formed the climax of his act, was also killed in the fire.

You've probably never heard of Colin T. Campbell, but for a decade this Edinburgh lad churned out silent movies in Hollywood, and his 1914 film *The Spoilers* was the first 'epic' in the American canon, leading directly to filmmakers wanting to make big, bigger and even bigger films.

The Last Emperor of China (1987) was based on the extraordinary experiences of Sir Reginald Johnston, who tutored Puyi, the last Chinese emperor, within the confines of the Forbidden City in Beijing from 1919 until the revolution of 1924. Johnston was born on Canaan Lane in Morningside in 1874 and studied at Edinburgh University. His book *Twilight in the Forbidden City* formed the basis for the film, in which he was played by Peter O'Toole.

The Singing Street (1951) is a charming evocation of children's singing games, all filmed in the back greens of Leith. Pure nostalgia combined with an anthropological eye for urban childhood customs.

The Edinburgh Film Festival, started in 1947, is the oldest continually running film festival in the world. It was first known as the International Festival of Documentary Film, even though feature films were also shown.

Opened in 1929 with a capacity exceeding 3,000, the Playhouse at the top of Leith Walk was the second largest cinema in Scotland. In

1969, when the counterculture biker film *Easy Rider* had its European premiere at the Playhouse, the movie's star Peter Fonda turned up, as did several dozen Hells' Angels, plus their bikes.

EDINBURGH SUBSTITUTING FOR OTHER PLACES ON SCREEN...

In *The Battle of the Sexes* (1959) Arthur's Seat stands in for the mountains of the West Highlands.

The 'ice fight' scene in the Glasgow urban youth drama *Small Faces* (1996) was filmed in Edinburgh's Murrayfield Ice Rink, with many of the regular skaters as extras.

Parts of *Mary Reilly* (1996), a re-telling of the Jekyll and Hyde story from a maidservant's point of view, were filmed in the Cowgate, substituting for London.

...AND OTHER PLACES PRETENDING TO BE EDINBURGH

In 1940 a German propaganda film claimed to show large fires in Edinburgh after a major bombing raid. In fact the damage had been relatively minor, while the footage was actually of the Luftwaffe's attack on Rotterdam.

The saccharine *Greyfriars Bobby* (1961) was mostly filmed in a studio. In *The Adventures of Greyfriars Bobby* (2005), Stirling Castle substituted for Edinburgh Castle – look out for a scene in which the iconic Wallace Monument, which towers over Stirling from a hill, can be clearly seen in the background. Elsewhere in this geographically-confused film, characters apparently crossing lowland East Lothian are seen passing mountains and lochs from the Scottish Highlands, which in reality are many miles distant in an entirely different part of the country.

In the excellent 1945 horror *The Body Snatcher* and the dire 'comedy' *Burke & Hare* (2010), Greyfriars Bobby (active 1860-1872) is anachronistically pitched into the world of bodysnatchers/murderers Burke and Hare (active 1828-29).

Some of the 'Edinburgh' urban scenes in *Restless Natives* (1985) were actually filmed in Glasgow, leading to an Edinburgh Corporation bus being imported into a Glaswegian housing scheme.

ACTORS AND ACTRESSES

A full list of Edinburgh actors would fill half this book. Here are just a few:

Alastair Sim, one of *the* great British actors of his time, was born in the city, and was even rector at the University of Edinburgh from 1948 to 1951. His most famous role was as Miss Fritton the St Trinians

HASELDEN.

headmistress (and her twin brother) in *The Belles of St Trinians* (1954) and *Blue Murder at St Trinians* (1957). As we have seen, the fictional St Trinians was partly based on a real-life Edinburgh school.

Ewen Bremner's gawky visage will be forever remembered as Spud in *Trainspotting*, but this fine actor has also appeared in dozens of other productions, often as a supporting role in US blockbusters such as *Black Hawk Down* and *Alien Vs. Predator*.

The late Ian Charleson was best known for portraying Olympic athlete Eric Liddell in *Chariots of Fire* (1981); he was also probably the best Shakespearean stage actor of his generation.

The terrific Hannah Gordon is seemingly ubiquitous on British television drama shows and sitcoms; she has a rose named after her.

Ian Richardson's apparently haughty demeanour meant he excelled at playing smooth but dangerous Establishment figures, none more so than his scheming Tory Prime Minister Frances Urquhart in the BBC series *House of Cards*. Richardson also portrayed both Sherlock Holmes and Joseph Bell, the Edinburgh doctor and proto-forensic scientist on whom Conan Doyle based his iconic detective.

For some, Ken Stott is the world-weary, lived-in television face of DI John Rebus, or forlorn hospital radio DJ Eddie McKenna from BBC Scotland's *Takin' Over the Asylum*; for others, perhaps of a younger generation, he is the dwarf Balin in *The Hobbit*.

If you've seen David Lean's epic 1946 version of *Great Expectations*, you will be unable to forget Finlay Currie as the terrifying convict Magwitch.

And talking of frightening screen incarnations, watch Iain Glen as the gangleader in the TV drama *The Fear* (1988). Brrrr.

Fountainbridge is the birthplace of Sir Sean Connery, arguably the most famous Scotsman in the world. Long before he set the film world on fire playing James Bond, however, Connery was the local milk delivery boy, before making use of his physique to become a model and bodybuilder (bronze medal winner in the 1950 Mr Universe contest, beefcake fans). In 1982 he returned to his native city for the documentary *Sean Connery's Edinburgh*, in which he explored his former haunts. A decade later he was made a freeman of the city.

A fellow Edinburgh actor, Anthony Dawson, played Professor Dent in Connery's first Bond film, *Dr. No* (1962).

ENTERTAINERS

Edinburgh, home to a legion of comedic talents during the Festival, is the native city of two of the best-loved comedians of British television, Ronnie Corbett and Rory Bremner.

The Edinburgh celebrity is Sir Harry Lauder, born in Portobello in 1870. At one point the highest-paid entertainer in the world, Lauder's appeal spanned generations, and he is best-known today for writing 'Keep Right on to the End of the Road'. The Portobello bypass is called Sir Harry Lauder Road, and a 'corkscrew' form of hazel is

known as Harry Lauder's Walking Stick because Lauder habitually appeared with a crooked walking stick.

Shirley Manson, singer with cult group Goodbye Mr Mackenzie and later the global-dominating alternative rockers Garbage, is a native of Edinburgh. Manson found a new audience when playing a businesswoman (actually a robot from the future) in the TV series *Terminator: The Sarah Connor Chronicles*.

Reggae artist Finley Quaye is a son of Leith.

'January' by Edinburgh group Pilot hit the Number One spot in January 1975.

Perhaps the most successful Edinburgh group were the Bay City Rollers, who from 1974 to 1976 sold millions of records, prompting scenes of teenage 'Rollermania'. There are undoubtedly a number of readers today who (fondly, or with embarrassment) remember wearing the fans' tartan 'uniform' of calf-length trousers and scarves.

13 WELL-KNOWN EDINBURGH MUSEUMS AND GALLERIES

Edinburgh is a city where cultural institutions are as plentiful as bagpiping buskers. These are thirteen of the best-known places to visit – all are excellent:

1. The National Museum of Scotland
2. The National Gallery of Scotland
3. The Royal Scottish Academy
4. The Scottish National Portrait Gallery
5. The Scottish National Gallery of Modern Art
6. The City Art Centre
7. The Museum of Edinburgh
8. The National War Museum of Scotland
9. The Museum of Childhood
10. The Writers' Museum
11. John Knox House
12. The People's Story Museum
13. The Camera Obscura

13 LESS WELL-KNOWN EDINBURGH MUSEUMS AND GALLERIES

There are also many other less-celebrated attractions, all of which are well worth the time to seek out and explore:

1. *The Edinburgh University Collection of Historic Musical Instruments*. This quirky collection comes in two parts.

The St Cecilia's Hall Museum of Instruments holds historic keyboard instruments (harpsichords, virginals, spinets, organs and so on) and plucked instruments (harps, lutes, citterns and guitars), all in an eighteenth-century auditorium on Cowgate which happens to be the oldest concert hall in Scotland (and the second oldest in Britain). The Reid Concert Hall Museum of Instruments, meanwhile, is a wonderfully old-fashioned Victorian collection of stringed, woodwind, brass and percussion instruments, on display in the Reid Concert Hall on Bristo Square. Limited opening hours in each case, but worth it.

2. *The Museum of Fire* is in a former fire station on Lauriston Place and celebrates the oldest fire brigade in the country, with some superb early fire engines (both motorized and horse-drawn).

3. *The Police Centre* on the Royal Mile is a small but perfectly formed museum. And it has displays on Deacon Brodie, Burke & Hare and other members of the Edinburgh gallery of rogues.

4. *The National Museums Collection Centre* in Granton is the place where the National Museums of Scotland store all the things they can't put on display, from dinosaur bones to traction engines. And sometimes you can visit it (pre-bookings only). If the opportunity presents itself, go.

5. *Trinity House Maritime Museum*, a Georgian neoclassical house opposite South Leith Parish Church, is the perfect place to explore Leith's seafaring past.

6. *Surgeons' Hall Museum* on Nicholson Street is perhaps not for the faint of heart or stomach, but its parade of diseased or damaged body parts, prosthetic limbs, surgical tools, masks to hide facial disfigurement, and other aspects of grue and gore make for a fascinatingly queasy visit. Watch out for some bits belonging to so-called bodysnatcher William Burke.

7. More body parts can be found at the Anatomical Museum of the School of Biomedical Sciences in the University of

Edinburgh. It's open to the public only occasionally, but is absolutely brilliant. Highlights include the skeletons of an elephant, a chimpanzee, the Cramond Murderer John Howison (the last criminal dissected after execution), and the notorious William Burke. The life mask of his partner William Hare is also here.

8. *The John Murray Archive Exhibition* at the National Library of Scotland is an interactive tour around the immense archive of one of the most important publishers in the English-speaking world. Some of Murray's authors included Charles Darwin, Lord Byron, David Livingstone and Sir Walter Scott, and documents and artefacts of these and seven other authors are on display.

9. *The Corstorphine Trust Museum* is one of those indispensable local museums, with displays on Corstorphine village's social history, personalities and environment. The museum and its associated archive is part of the Corstorphine Heritage Centre, situated in a beautifully-restored sixteenth-century crow-stepped house in St Margaret's Park.

10. If you want to get a feel for the New Town at its fashionable height in the late eighteenth century, visit *The Georgian House* at No. 7 Charlotte Square. Designed in 1791 by the foremost architect of the period, Robert Adam, this is the place to breathe refined, elegant, wealthy living.

11. *Gladstone's Land* on the Lawnmarket is the perfect companion to the Georgian House. This restored tenement gives a detailed insight into the indignities and discomforts of living in an upmarket address in the Old Town in the seventeenth century. The two houses together give a powerful sense of 'Edinburgh as two cities'.

12. *The Museum on The Mound* is all about money. One display even shows £1 million pounds in used £20 notes. The museum is inside the grandiose headquarters of the Bank of Scotland, itself a reason to visit, and until 2006 you could only get in here by making an appointment in advance. Now, visitors are invited

to try and crack open a safe, while the displays on crime and security are sobering.

13. *The National Museum of Flight.* Not strictly within Edinburgh, as it's a few miles east at East Fortune, but where else can you see a Concorde on the site of a former First World War airfield?

7

THE NATURAL WORLD

EARTHQUAKES

Minor earth tremors hit Edinburgh on 8 November 1608 and 30 September 1789. A three-second quake on 7 September 1801 killed two female shearers when a barn collapsed and caused a tenement in Paterson's Court off Barony Street to sink so much into the ground that the tenants were evacuated. Most of the shock was felt in the New Town, where the houses were 'lifted up gently, and then violently shaken in a direction from north to south,' as the *Scots Magazine* reported.

On 18 January 1889 an earthquake with a maximum intensity of 5 on the Richter Scale was felt across much of Edinburgh. The epicentre was several miles to the southwest.

As monitoring equipment has increased in sensitivity, so too have records of small earth tremors, with reports in 1972, 1977, 1978, 1979, 1981, 1996 and 1997, all concentrated on the eastern edge of the city.

In March 2011 some residents in Portobello thought an earthquake was shaking their houses. It turned out the vibrations were caused by the large vehicles shifting sand for a flood defence scheme.

THE ROCKS REMAIN

The Agassiz Rock in Blackford Quarry is venerated by geologists worldwide as a monument to the world-changing ideas of Louis Agassiz (1807-1873). The Swiss geologist advanced the then-revolutionary theory that the world had seen numerous Ice Ages, and that the action of the vanished ice could be detected on existing rocks. On 7 October 1840 *The Scotsman* published Agassiz's declaration that Scotland had once lain under a sheet of glaciers; and on 27 October he visited Blackford Hill, examined the rocks of the quarry, and told the accompanying party of Scottish geologists, 'That is the work of ice!'

Other clear glacial striations can be viewed on the western slopes of Corstorphine Hill, behind Edinburgh Zoo.

Edinburgh-born James Hutton (1726-1797) is credited with the then equally world-changing idea that the rocks of the earth were laid down at different periods, many having been created during ancient volcanic activity. He identified an example of once-molten volcanic rock protruding through older layers of sedimentary rocks on Salisbury Crags, a spot still known as Hutton's Section. Unfortunately Hutton's prose style was so dense that it needed later geologists to properly clarify and disseminate his ideas after his death. Hutton's pioneering research has enabled the University of Edinburgh to describe itself as 'the Birthplace of Geosciences', while Our Dynamic Earth, which tells the story of our planet's dramatic evolution from the Big Bang to the volcanoes, glaciers and rainforests of the present day, is one of the city's most popular attractions.

VOLCANOES

With a height of 823ft (251m), the long-extinct volcano of Arthur's Seat dominates the skyline. Volcanologists can distinguish remains of the volcano's cone, along with lava flows, ash deposits and other evidence that this part of Edinburgh was once molten rock.

Salisbury Crags, which extend to the south, are a *sill*, a horizontal sheet of magma that appeared underground even when the volcano itself was extinct. Erosion by ice has exposed the once-liquid magma to plain sight.

The Arthur's Seat volcano had four *vents*, holes where lava erupted, but which were not themselves as powerful as the main cone. One of the vents is the hill on which sits Edinburgh Castle. During the

last Ice Age, the glaciers coming from the west were deflected by the hard rock of Castle Hill and flowed round to either side, creating the shallow valleys of Cowgate/the Grassmarket to the south and Princes Street Gardens on the north side. East of the castle, the Royal Mile slopes down a *tail* of softer rock which escaped the glaciers because the *crag* of Castle Hill blocked their path.

Crag-and-tail volcanic hills can be found all over Edinburgh, from Corstorphine Hill in the west to Blackford Hill in the south. Each has a plug of hard volcanic rock on the west side, a sloping tail of softer rocks to the east, and shallow ice-gouged valleys on the north and south sides.

EDINBURGH, THE GREEN CITY

41 per cent of the land within the boundaries of the City of Edinburgh is designated as greenbelt.

Taking into account all the parks, golf courses, allotments, school playing fields, private estates and other similar sites, there are 315 'green spaces' scattered throughout the city. This figure excludes all the thousands of household gardens.

A survey from 1957 showed that the city boundaries encompassed 52 farms, 120 market gardens, 37 piggeries and 17 smallholdings.

By 1995 many of these had disappeared, although there were still 31 farms in operation.

In 2004 the wild plant conservation charity Plantlife asked each county to nominate its representative flower. Edinburgh's choice was the sticky catchfly (*Lychnis viscaria*), a spectacular red flower that can be seen growing in clumps in Holyrood Park. It also used to grow on Castle Rock.

PARKS AND GARDENS

A 'physic garden', designed to grow plants of medicinal use, was established at St Anne's Yard near Holyrood Palace in 1670. Having relocated to just off Leith Walk in 1763, the continually-expanding garden moved to its present home in Inverleith in 1820, where it is now known as the Royal Botanic Garden Edinburgh, or simply 'The Botanics'. And magnificent it is too.

The garden now holds over 30,000 separate plants representing almost 15,000 species. Specimens of about 5 per cent of the world's entire plant species are held. It is a major global player in plant conservation.

'The Botanics' is a hugely popular attraction, especially with families. To see every planted section and glasshouse on the site would take an entire summer's day, from dawn to sundown, without pausing for breaks.

The Palm House is the tallest in the United Kingdom.

The Botanics' Herbarium holds 3 million specimens of dried plants, collected from the seventeenth century to the present day, and representing around half of all the plants in the world. Amongst this leading international research collection are plants obtained by Charles Darwin on his voyage to South America.

If you want something less grandiose, head to Dunbar's Close near Canongate churchyard, where a tiny oasis open to the public recreates the flowers, herbs and style of a seventeenth-century garden.

Even more special is Dr Neil's Garden in Duddingston, where for almost forty years general practitioners Andrew and Nancy Neil laboured to create a garden out of nothing. This genuine 'secret garden' is open to the public, and many people find it has a meditative, almost spiritual quality.

The largest skateboarding park in Scotland can be found in Saughton Park.

The present Craigmillar Country Park used to be home to the Danger Woods, so-called because they stored the remaining products of the site's former gunpowder works.

SIGNIFICANT TREES

In 2002 the Forestry Commission identified Scotland's top 100 'heritage trees' – trees with a particular natural, cultural or historical heritage. By 2006 the list had grown to 130, members of the public having contributed additional suggestions. Six of these heritage trees are in the Edinburgh area:

1. *The Corstorphine Sycamore*, at the corner of North Saughton Road and Dovecot Road, was around 400 years old when it

was blown down in the catastrophic Boxing Day gale of 1998. A landmark for centuries, it was associated with a crime of passion (a woman killed her lover beneath its branches) as well as a legend of buried treasure and a guardian ghost. The stump of the great tree lasted until 2005, by which time the salvaged timber had been made into a variety of artefacts – clocks, turned bowls and eggcups – as well as an exceptionally fine violin, which is reserved for gifted musicians at St Mary's Music School. A descendent of the original Corstorphine Sycamore can be seen in the churchyard of Corstorphine Kirk.

2. *The Four Disciples*, in the walled Malleny Garden, Balerno. These four clipped yews were probably planted around 1635, and were originally part of a group of twelve, said to represent the Disciples of Jesus. The other eight trees were, sadly, felled by the property owner in 1961. The garden is now in the care of the National Trust for Scotland and is open to all.

3. *The Royal Botanic Gardens Silver Birch*, an amazingly twisted nineteenth-century specimen that has survived to twice the age of most birch trees in the wild.

4. *Stevenson's Yew* in Colinton. This magnificent yew beside Colinton Church Manse formed part of Robert Louis Stevenson's childhood playground – in his book *Memories and Portraits* Stevenson described 'the great yew making elsewhere a pleasing horror of shade.' The tree was already old in 1630, when it was recorded in the minutes of the local Kirk Session.

5. *The Roslin Sweet Chestnut*, a vast and contorted 450-year-old tree about 500 yards from mysterious Rosslyn Chapel.

6. *The Comiston House Austrian Pine* on Camus Avenue. This was probably planted in the late 1830s, making it one of the earliest examples in the UK. Having been saved from the developers' chainsaws, its distinctive forked shape is now the logo of the Fairmilehead Association, whose members campaigned to spare the tree.

Other significant trees can be found dotted around Edinburgh:

The five monkey puzzle trees at Lauriston Castle are probably some of the oldest in the UK. *Araucaria araucana* was introduced into Britain from its native Chile in 1795, and the Lauriston specimens are believed to date from very early in the nineteenth century.

The Camperdown Elm near to the main door of St Cuthbert's Church at the west end of Princes Street is the largest specimen in Scotland in terms of girth.

The tallest trees in Edinburgh can be found in The Hermitage of Braid woodland in the south of the city, where several specimens of beech, ash and sycamore are more than 130ft (40m) in height.

In 1935, 5,000 Girl Guides marked the Silver Jubilee of King George V by planting more than 400 cherry trees in Braidburn Valley Park. The trees were arranged in a shape of a trefoil, the Guides' emblem.

Over three days in October 1997, the 'Edinburgh Plantathon' saw 39,650 trees planted as part of the Craigmillar Urban Forest Project.

One particular tree of significance was blown down in 1819. The sycamore that used to flourish in the cloister of Holyrood Abbey was planted by Mary, Queen of Scots, the young tree having been brought by Mary from France.

THE ANIMAL KINGDOM

Edinburgh is no wildlife desert. Ninety species of birds have been recorded in the city, along with roe deer, otters, hares and five types of bat. There are also thirty-seven different spider species lurking in darkened spaces.

Dolphins can sometimes be seen from Silverknowes.

Urban cemeteries may not be the first place you think of when it comes to spotting wildlife, but the mature trees and overgrown verdure of Warriston Cemetery make it a natural haven, with a top predator at the peak of the foodchain – the sparrowhawk.

In 1688 the much-admired mute swans of Duddingston Loch triggered a legal ownership dispute between the Duchess of Lauderdale and Sir James Dick of Prestonfield. When the court ruled in favour of the former, Sir James evicted the swans from the loch. Fortunately they have since returned.

When the New Town was under construction, the workmen set snares in the adjacent fields, dining on rabbits, hares, and the occasional pheasant belonging to the Earl of Moray. The first residents of Charlotte Square could hear the distinctive sound of corncrakes from their houses. These days the Scottish population of corncrakes is largely confined to the west coast and islands.

Large numbers of urban foxes are now resident in the city. A study from 1984 showed that dog foxes could have a territory of 4.5km², while vixens had a typical range of 1.5km², as they did not move far from their cubs. Dog foxes tended to use disused railway lines to get around.

In November and December 2008 foxes were seen fearlessly entering shops on Princes Street and the Royal Mile during daylight. Other shops reported persistent customers such as a black-backed gull and a pigeon with one leg.

Urban foxes have now become characters in Edinburgh fiction: Brother Fox is a frequent visitor to Isabel Dalhousie's garden in Alexander McCall Smith's series of novels starting with *The Sunday Philosophy Club* (2004).

In 1954 the American movie star Roy Rogers stayed at the Caledonian Hotel, and was photographed leading his famous steed, Trigger the Wonder Horse, up the Caley's grand staircase. Contrary to the story fed to the press, Trigger did not stay in a hotel room, but in a stable.

While in residence at Holyrood Palace Mary, Queen of Scots enjoyed archery, bowls, tennis and hawking. Holyrood Park did not have enough game for hunting with horses and hounds, however, so wild boars were imported from France.

Dr Munro, one of the founders of the Medical School, taught his parrot to sing the National Anthem. During the physician's extended absence, his wife, an avowed Jacobite, always silenced the patriotic parrot with a cry of, 'Hush, you rogue!' Thereafter whenever Dr Munro attempted to sing 'God Save the King', the bird cried out, 'Hush, you rogue!'

Visitors to the stinking, refuse-strewn Old Town were sometimes surprised to encounter pigs in cellars and even dwelling houses. In the mid-nineteenth century Dr Thomas Guthrie, the Moderator

of the Free Church of Scotland, came across a huge porker in an upper tenement room on the Cowgate, and asked how the lumbering beast had got up the narrow winding staircase. The owner told him this had never been a problem. When Dr Guthrie enquired further, he was told the pig had been born and had lived its entire life in the apartment.

The Scottish Society for Prevention of Cruelty to Animals was established at Edinburgh in 1839.

GREYFRIARS BOBBY

Greyfriars Bobby is arguably the most famous dog in the world – and undoubtedly the most photographed, as his statue on Candlemaker Row is on every tourist itinerary. The story of how the faithful dog watched over his master's grave, shivering through the Scottish winter, captivated Victorian audiences, and led to a highly sentimental novel and two equally glutinous films.

Recent research by author Jan Bondeson has removed the layers of legend and clarified the facts. Bobby did live in Greyfriars graveyard, but he did not pine over a grave, for his master was not buried there. Indeed, no one knows who his master was. The little dog did not keep to the graveyard 24/7, and roamed around the area, being temporarily fed and sheltered in a variety of homes. In 1867 Bobby died. Such was his fame, however – a fame that benefited the local commercial establishments – that a substitute dog was quickly found. Greyfriars Bobby Mark I was an elderly terrier mongrel, while Greyfriars Bobby Mark II was a Skye terrier of the same size but with a slightly different coloured coat. The latter dog died in 1872.

The iconic statue, the subject of millions of tourist photographs, is of Greyfriars Bobby Mark II – the substitute dog.

BOTANY AND ZOOLOGY IN THE STREETS

The Wisp means a small set of trees. Other tree-related street names include Beggars Bush, Bush Street, Guardianswood, March

Pines, Orchard Brae, Shrub Mount, The Spinney and Timber Bush. More conventionally, we find roads named after Beech, Birch, Blackthorn, Blaeberry, Bramble, Hawthorn, Hazel, Juniper, Larch, Laurel, Lime, Myrtle, Oak, Poplar, Rowan, Spruce, Sycamore, Willow and Yew.

Cockit Hat (the Scots term for a cocked hat, or tricorn) is the name of a triangle of woodland in Oxgangs.

Townwomen's Guild Walk in the Meadows is lined with trees planted on behalf of the guild in 1973.

The 'Hyvot' in Hyvot Avenue is a corruption of 'Heavy Oats', a reference to the farm that once stood here.

The animal kingdom is represented by Cowgate, Dolphin Road, Hares Close, Fox Spring Rise, Fox Covert Grove, and Horse Wynd. Cuddy Lane uses the Scots word for horse or pony. Hart Street refers to a young stag.

Pennywell Cottages at the junction of West Granton Road and Marine Drive is another animal-related name. When small ponies from Orkney and Shetland unloaded at Granton, destined for the coal mines, the first spot the drovers could water the animals was at the well here, for which they paid a fee of one penny.

In myth salamanders were believed to live in fire; and a suitably fiery glass and chemical works once existed on Salamander Street. The city's only dragon is at Wyvern Park (a wyvern is a two-legged dragon).

As well as Falcon Avenue, bird names include Hawkhill, Peacocktail Close, Ravenshaugh Road, Ravenswood Avenue, Sandpiper Road, Swan Crescent and Swan Spring Avenue. Laverockbank Road refers to laverocks or larks, and Caponhall Road to chickens. Crows appear in Corbiehill, Corbiewynd and Corbieshot (the suffix '-shot' referred to a strip of land, often on a spur of rock).

Parrotshot in Duddingston sounds like it belongs in a Monty Python sketch.

ZOOS AND MENAGERIES

Holyrood Palace, like many of the residences of European royalty, had its own menagerie, populated by exotic animals that were usually gifts to the king. The records are unclear, but there appears to have been a tiger and possibly a lion here in the time of James IV, while James V had an ape and James VI a camel. Other animals known to have lived at the Palace included lynx and bears. We do not know how well these creatures were cared for.

The first Edinburgh Zoological Gardens opened in Broughton in 1839, occupying a site bounded by what is now the built-up area of East Claremont Street, West Annandale Street, Bellevue Road and Melgund Terrace.

The zoo's leading light was Patrick Neill, one of Edinburgh's most dynamic intellectual eccentrics – amongst other things, he was an expert horticulturalist and antiquarian, designed the layout for West Princes Street Gardens, and promoted the draining of the Nor' Loch. His personal garden in Canonmills contained over 3,000 plants (many of them exotic) in a variety of greenhouses, and he shared his home with a menagerie of parrots, cockatoos and cats.

The Broughton Park Zoo housed mammals and birds, as well as the skeleton of a blue whale (which is still on display in the Royal Scottish Museum on Chambers Street). In 1855 the zoo was sold to a carnival. The animals were displayed in poor conditions, succumbed to disease, and the enterprise closed down in 1857.

Travelling menageries and showmen often visited with 'unusual' animals captured in the expanding British Empire. In December 1835 a male Indian Rhinoceros was on display at 13 South St David Street. Admittance was one shilling (half price for children and tradespeople). The animal was described in *The Scotsman* as having 'a coat of mail so hard as to resist the effect of a musket shot.' In February 1836 a heavy snowfall blocked the roads and postponed the celebrated rhino's scheduled departure for Glasgow.

In 1872 a bull Asian elephant named Maharajah was bought at auction in Edinburgh, for delivery to Belle Vue Zoo in Manchester, a distance of over 250 miles. Maharajah and his handler walked all the way.

Edinburgh antiquarian Sir John Graham Dalyell (1775-1851), author of zoological works such as *The Powers of the Creator displayed in the Creation* and *Rare and Remarkable Animals of Scotland*, researched his books by studying marine animals at his home in Edinburgh. Three times a week a servant was dispatched to the seashore to haul up four gallons of seawater to refresh the tanks.

Somewhere near what is now Princes Mall stood a Victorian aquarium and seal-pond, part of the aggrandised vegetable market building that once operated opposite St Andrew Street.

The present Edinburgh Zoo has been on its Corstorphine Hill site since its foundation in 1913. When it first opened it did not own many animals and so hired some from Sir Garrard Tyrwhitt-Drake, who had the largest private zoo in Britain.

Edinburgh was the first zoo in the world to house and breed penguins, and a penguin still features on the zoo's crest.

In 1950 an open gate at the pool led to an accidental penguin promenade. The sight attracted so much attention that a daily Penguin Parade around the zoo was inaugurated, a tradition maintained every summer afternoon to this day.

Sir Nils Olav is the only penguin in the world with a knighthood. The mascot of the Norwegian Guard, he started off as a mere Lance-Corporal, but was quickly fast-tracked through the ranks, becoming Sergeant Major and then Colonel. The resident of Edinburgh Zoo was knighted in 2008, by approval of the King of Norway. As with Greyfriars Bobby, the current Nils is a substitute, the original penguin having died in 1987.

From the start, the zoo concentrated on breeding its animals, scoring early successes with sea lions, beavers, orang-utans and of course penguins. In 1938 it celebrated the birth of its first wolf litter – but three years later the wolves were euthanised, as it was feared that bombing might let them escape and be a danger to the population. The decision was probably prompted when a bomb killed six budgerigars and damaged the reptile and ape houses on 4 November 1940.

One of the zoo's most famous residents was Wojtek the Soldier Bear, a Syrian Brown Bear cub adopted by the men of the 22nd Company Polish Army Service and Corps (Artillery) in 1943. On active service at the Battle of Monte Cassino in Italy, Wojtek – who had his own soldier's rank and number – helped carry boxes of artillery shells

while under enemy fire. He lived out his latter years at the zoo, responding whenever he heard Polish spoken on visits by his former comrades-in-arms, and enjoying the cigarettes they threw to him. Wojtek died in 1963.

In 2005 the zoo opened the Living Links to Human Evolution Centre, Britain's first research centre dedicated to primate behaviour and psychology, which also has a chimpanzee observation facility.

The zoo is the only one in the UK that houses giant pandas and koalas.

THE WEATHER

Robert Louis Stevenson famously described Edinburgh as having 'one of the vilest climates under heaven.'

The full quote, which is from his 1879 book *Edinburgh: Picturesque Notes*, goes on: 'She is liable to be beaten upon by all the winds that blow, to be drenched with rain, to be buried in cold sea fogs out of the

east, and powdered with the snow as it comes flying southward from the Highland hills. The weather is raw and boisterous in winter, shifty and ungenial in summer, and a downright meteorological purgatory in the spring.' Stevenson concludes his tirade with an ominous warning: 'The delicate die early.'

English visitor Edward Topham thought that the city's worst feature was its winds. In *Letters from Edinburgh* (1776) he noted how front doors of houses in the New Town needed three or four people to close them against the wind; how sedan chairs were often overturned; and how eddies between the buildings, by gathering up dust and stones, could make it impossible to venture out of doors.

On average, it rains in Edinburgh for 191 days every year, or sixteen days per month. In recent years the longest period without any rain was nineteen days.

The coldest temperature ever recorded in Edinburgh was -17°C, while the hottest was 31°C. July and August temperatures rarely top 22°C.

In Paul Johnston's novel *Water of Death*, Edinburgh in 2025 is suffering a heatwave and drought caused by global warming.

The sunniest year in the past half-century was 1995, while the darkest year was 1983. 17 per cent of all Edinburgh days have no sunshine at all.

2008 was the wettest year, where the rainfall was 41 per cent higher than average. In August of that year the rainfall was 226 per cent higher than the usual readings for the month.

8

SPORTS AND GAMES

ARCHERY

The Royal Company of Archers was founded in Edinburgh in 1676; since 1822 it has also had a ceremonial role, that of the Queen's (or King's) Bodyguard in Scotland, which means they have to be present for State or other royal occasions. The Royal Company is required, on request, to present three barbed arrows to the Queen.

The Edinburgh Arrow, an archery prize, was presented by the city in 1709 and has been the subject of an annual competition ever since.

ATHLETICS, WALKING & RUNNING

Supervised student sports and games had been taking place on the Borough Muir since the fifteenth century. By the eighteenth century a new pastime emerged – pedestrianism, or professional footracing, an early version of what is now called power walking. In 1794 American medical student Ephraim McDowell competed against one of his colleagues at Edinburgh for the fastest walk over 60 yards. McDowell came second, forfeiting 10 guineas, but then promptly challenged the winner for a rematch over 100 yards, this time raising the stakes to a phenomenal 100 guineas. The wily McDowell had deliberately lost the first race, and, in a classic sting, won the second race and walked away, literally, with about £6,000 in today's money.

Sometime in the early years of the nineteenth century a Highland teenager walked, for a bet, from Edinburgh to Glasgow and back again, accomplishing the feat in twenty-four hours. Sir John McNeill, as he later became, went on to be the British Empire's fixer in Persia, taking part in the 'Great Game' against the imperial ambitions of Russia.

Pedestrianism reached its peak with the inauguration in 1870 of the New Year Sprint at Powderhall in Edinburgh, where 'peds' of all classes competed for cash prizes. The Sprint has been held every year since, although from 1999 the venue has been Musselburgh. Entrants for the 110m walk are 'handicapped' – varied in their

starting point, depending on their ability – thus ensuring close finishes. The Sprint is unique, the last survivor of the once-popular pedestrianist galas.

One of the endlessly-sprouting gentlemen's clubs of the Georgian period was the Six Foot Club, where men of the requisite stature practiced 'the national games of Scotland' – hammer throwing, quoits, triple jumping and steeplechasing – at Hunters' Tryst, near Oxgangs.

The Six Foot Club often attracted positive press attention, as in 1828 when the *Edinburgh Examiner* enthusiastically reported on a steeplechase. According to the account, this particular mile-long uphill cross-country run was won by Royal Navy officer Archibald Sinclair – in three and a half minutes, no less. Either Mr Sinclair was an athletic prodigy the like of which has never been seen since, or the journalist got his facts wrong, as the current world record for running a mile *on the flat* is three minutes and forty-three seconds.

During the winter months the Six Foot Club convened at premises in East Thistle Street or Malta Terrace, and on these convivial occasions we find distinguished but distinctly non-athletic honorary members present, such as Sir Walter Scott, who was not only well below 6ft, but lame to boot.

In 1828 the Six Foot Club, in their dress uniform, acted as an impressive Guard of Honour to the Lord High Constable of Scotland.

Edinburgh's fee-paying schools and its university played a major role in the development of sporting activities in the city during Victorian times, partly as the consequence of a 'fit body, fit mind' ethos that permeated the British Empire. In 1858 Edinburgh Academy became the first school in the city with an annual sports day, with Merchiston Castle School and the Royal High School of Edinburgh following over the next few years. As the scholars of the public schools entered the university, so the demand for sports there increased. The University Athletic Club was founded in 1865, leading to its first sports day at Greenhill Park on 27 June 1866 (the first such university event outside Oxford and Cambridge).

Five years later the first Scottish inter-university competition took place at the Edinburgh Academicals ground on Raeburn Place.

The university's most famous athlete was Eric Liddell, who won the gold medal for the 400m race at the Paris Olympics in 1924, setting a world record of 47.6 seconds. A devout Christian, Liddell had previously withdrawn from the 100m sprint, his best event, because the heats were held on a Sunday.

The model for the statue on the dome of the University Old Quad off South Bridge was student (and professional athlete) Anthony Hall.

Powderhall was the venue for the city's first non-university athletics championships, held on 23 June 1883.

The principal athletics venue today is Meadowbank Stadium, which hosted the Commonwealth Games in 1970 and 1986.

Alan Wells from Liberton topped a stellar athletics career with a gold medal for the 100m sprint at the 1980 Moscow Olympics.

The Edinburgh Marathon, a 26-mile run through the city and East Lothian, has been an annual event since 2003. In the first year, entrant Lloyd Stott took more than six days to complete the course, possibly because he was wearing 100lb of deep-sea diving suit.

BASEBALL

There are currently three baseball teams in the city – the Edinburgh Diamond Devils, the Edinburgh Cannons and the Edinburgh Giants. The game appears to have been introduced to Scotland by visiting American airmen.

BOWLS

A form of bowls was played at Holyrood Palace in 1501, the bowler-in-chief being King James IV.

In 1691 the Merchants Company of Edinburgh built a bowling green off Cowgate, but they had to wait another two years for their bowls to arrive from London. The game took off, and private and family bowling greens sprouted around the Royal Mile.

The semi-public Tamson's Green was in use for seventy-five years from 1692. When it closed in 1768 two greens were laid out in the grounds of George Heriot's Hospital. The following year the Society of Bowlers was incorporated, with forty members.

The oldest recorded bowling club in the city is the Edinburgh Bowling Club (formerly Archers' Hall Bowling Club), formed in 1848; the club's unofficial prehistory stretches as far back as 1791.

There are currently seventy-seven bowls clubs in the city.

BOXING

Leith lad Tom Imrie won the light middleweight gold medal at the 1970 Commonwealth Games, the venue being the indoor arena at Murrayfield.

The same year, Ken Buchanan became the World Lightweight Boxing Champion. In 1978 *Boxing News* voted him the greatest-ever British boxer. A documentary on Buchanan, *The Boxer from Somewhere Else*, was released in 2012.

COCKFIGHTING

This cruel and now thankfully illegal sport was once hugely popular with all levels of society. A cockfighting pit was in operation on Leith Links in 1702.

CRICKET

Scotland may not be one of the foremost cricketing nations but the sport has always been popular in well-heeled Edinburgh and the national team is based at the Grange Club in Stockbridge.

CROQUET

Meadows Croquet Club, at the west end of the Meadows, is the home of the National Croquet Centre.

CROSS-COUNTRY RUNNING

Edinburgh Harriers were formed in 1885. Unusually egalitarian for the period, the club's members included both university-educated urban professionals and working-class men. Their first run, over a trail of 6 miles, was from the Harp Hotel in Corstorphine, and they later branched out to the entire city, sometime travelling to the starting point by train. In their early days the runners faced difficulties with barbed-wire fences and armed (and trespass-minded) landowners.

CURLING AND ICE SPORTS

The Edinburgh Skating Club, founded in 1742 or 1744, was the first organised figure skating club in the world. Its members practiced choreographed group skating on Duddingston Loch.

The Haymarket Ice Rink used to stand close to Haymarket Station but was closed in 1978, having hosted ice skating and curling for sixty-six years. These days all ice sports, including ice hockey, are concentrated at Murrayfield Ice Rink, the largest permanently seated indoor arena in Scotland. Murrayfield's scheduled opening in 1939 was cancelled because of the outbreak of war, and the venue was requisitioned for the Royal Army Service Corps. The rink finally opened to the public in 1952. The flexibility of the venue has also seen it used for boxing matches, music concerts, and appearances by the Harlem Globetrotters basketball show.

'Winter Wonderland' is a temporary outdoor ice rink set up every year in East Princes Street Gardens during the city's Christmas festival. Hugely popular, with a spectacular setting, it is also the place where hundreds of future couples either met or went on their first date together.

CYCLING

Edinburgh Racing Club was founded in 1925 and is still going strong.

The city has a number of traffic-free cycle routes, frequently running along old railway lines, and the National Cycle Network and the North Sea Cycle Route run through Edinburgh.

FOOTBALL

Edinburgh has two principal clubs in Edinburgh, Heart of Midlothian FC and Hibernian FC, 'Hearts' and 'Hibs' respectively. The former appear to be named directly after Sir Walter Scott's *Heart of Midlothian*, but it seems the name came from a dance hall, the name of which was taken from Scott's classic novel.

Hearts were founded in 1874, playing first on The Meadows. After several moves they ended up in Gorgie, and have been there ever since 1881. They first played at Tynecastle Stadium, their present venue, in 1886.

Tynecastle's record attendance came on 13 February 1932, when 53,396 people watched Hearts lose 1-0 to Rangers in a Scottish Cup match. After a great many changes, the stadium's current capacity is 17,420.

Hibs also started off playing on The Meadows, having been formed the year after Hearts started. They had the usual round of numerous different venues and financial difficulties, and even vanished for a year, before finally settling in 1892 on Easter Road in Leith.

The attendance record at Easter Road stands at 65,860, for a local derby with Hearts on 2 January 1950 (Hearts won 2-1). This is the largest crowd for any football match ever played in Edinburgh. The current capacity is 20,421.

In 1881 Hibernian Park, the predecessor to Easter Road, saw the world's first women's international football match, Scotland beating England 3-0. Things weren't what they seemed, however, as all the players from both sides were actually members of the same club in Glasgow.

From the start, Hibernian FC was focused on the immigrant Catholic community, while Hearts were always identified with the Protestant majority. Although supporters of both Hibs and Hearts sometimes maintain a religious solidarity today, the feeling is nowhere as intense as the sectarian hatred that disfigures football in Glasgow.

Edinburgh's *other* football club, now no longer in the city, started in 1943 as the works team of the Ferranti engineering factory, graduating to semi-professional status as Ferranti Thistle. In 1974 the club joined the Scottish Football League, but was forced to change its name because of the ban on overt name sponsorship. The newly-christened Meadowbank Thistle operated out of Meadowbank Stadium for twenty years, before relocating to Livingston in West Lothian in 1995 and undergoing another name-change, this time to Livingston FC.

GOLF

Tobias Smollett's comic novel from 1771, *The Expedition of Humphry Clinker*, contains a description of 'a game called golf' in Edinburgh, in which the players used clubs tipped with horn to strike 'small elastic balls of leather, stuffed with feathers.'

No one really knows how long golf has been played in Edinburgh, but the Burgess Golfing Society of Edinburgh started as early as 1735 and claims to be the oldest golfing society in the world (it became 'The Royal Burgess' in 1929). The Company of Edinburgh Golfers, another early foundation, dates its history back to 1744.

The Burgess Society started life on Bruntsfield Links, southwest of The Meadows. The Links is the oldest short-hole golf course in the world, and is the last vestige of the Borough Muir, the open space once used for everything from quarantine camps to public executions. The Bruntsfield Links Society was founded in 1761, sharing the Links with the Burgess Society until the latter moved out to Musselburgh Links in 1874 and then Barnton two decades later.

According to Smollett, the game was popular with all ranks of life. One quartet he mentioned was notable for having played the game their entire lives – and the youngest of the four was more than eighty years old.

Around 1906 a similar foursome played a match at Musselburgh – the combined age of the players was 340 years, giving the quartet an average age of eighty-five.

There are currently more than twenty golf courses within the city limits.

In what may be one of the great golfing stories of all time, an eighteenth-century player wagered that he could hit a ball from St Giles' Cathedral to the top of Arthur's Seat in just six strokes. According to the legend, he won his bet.

GREYHOUND RACING

Powderhall Stadium in Broughton hosted greyhound racing for almost seventy years before its closure in 1995. The site is now a housing estate.

HORSE RACING

In the later eighteenth century races were held on the shore at Leith for a week each summer. The historian Hugo Arnot noted that the sands were 'heavy and fatiguing for the horses, especially if they are not of strong bottom'. The races were hugely popular, and the maximum prize was 100 guineas.

Musselburgh Racecourse started up in 1816. During the racing season, the number of female 'escorts' in Glasgow and Newcastle dropped considerably, as all the ladies headed for Edinburgh to provide company for the 'swells' of high society. For those of more modest means, the races provided a cheap day out when trams started running directly to the racecourse from Waterloo Place. Musselburgh continues to host both Flat and Jump racing.

RUGBY

27 March 1871, Raeburn Place, Inverleith: the first international rugby game in the world, played between Scotland and England (Scotland won 4-1).

21 March 1925, Murrayfield, Roseburn: the first international rugby game in the Scottish Rugby Union's brand-new stadium, played between Scotland and England (Scotland won 14-11).

1 March 1975, Murrayfield Stadium: 104,000 people, the largest crowd ever to attend a rugby game in the UK, watched a Five Nations match played between Scotland and Wales (Scotland won 12-10).

It's fair to say that Scottish rugby has not always been as successful as on these occasions, but Murrayfield Stadium, the largest stadium in Scotland and one of the largest in the UK, remains at the heart of the game, and is home to both the national side and Edinburgh Rugby Club.

Gavin Hastings, former Scottish Rugby Captain and lead contender for the best Scottish rugby player ever, was born in Edinburgh.

SPEEDWAY

Somewhere between Meadowbank Stadium and the Meadowbank Velodrome there used to be a motorcycle speedway track called Old Meadowbank. The thrills 'n' spills sport started up here in 1948 and, after an on-off history, finally ceased in 1967; no trace of the stadium now remains. After a decade the sport returned to Edinburgh, this time at Powderhall Stadium, the races continuing until 1995.

In 1963 World Champion Peter Craven was killed at Old Meadowbank when he swerved to avoid a fallen rider and crashed into the trackside fence.

SWIMMING AND BATHING

In the nineteenth century summer sea-bathing became popular at Granton, Seafield, and Portobello. The city's first public swimming pools, which often incorporated baths for those who had no such facility at home, were opened in the 1860s, with examples in Pitt Street in Goldenacre and the South Back of Canongate, while another opened in 1884 on Nicholson Square on the site of the former Royal Infirmary.

Portobello Baths opened in 1901, and is home to the Portobello Water Polo Club, one of the most successful clubs in the UK.

The Warrender Private Baths opened in Marchmont in 1887, its upmarket facilities featuring a billiard room and reading room. The company suffered a financial reverse and the baths were bought by the city, where they are now the home of the Warrender Baths Club, perhaps the oldest swimming club in Scotland. The Club's alumni have included several Olympic athletes, including David Wilkie, Gold Medal winner at the Montreal Olympics in 1976. The Warrender Swim Centre, as it is officially known, is 'B' listed because of its glorious Victorian architecture.

9

EDINBURGH AT WORK AND PLAY

A WORKING CAPITAL

As the capital and a centre of learning and finance, Edinburgh has always had a significant professional sector, with a higher concentration of lawyers, bankers, academics, churchmen and doctors than anywhere else in Scotland. This then contrasts with the majority of the population, the urban working class, who feature far less in the standard story told of Edinburgh than their equivalents in, say, Glasgow.

In the 1690s the most visible and wealthy professional class in Glasgow were merchants; in Edinburgh it was lawyers.

The relatively large number of professionals in the city created a curious gender imbalance. So many women arrived in Edinburgh to work as domestic servants that, for decades, females outnumbered males three to two in the population.

SOME STATISTICS ABOUT EDINBURGH'S ECONOMY
(WHICH ARE ACTUALLY QUITE INTERESTING)

In 2011 Edinburgh's economic output was estimated at £16.7 billion. This was the second highest UK per capita figure outside of London.

This economic strength is the result of 258,300 people (72 per cent of adults between the ages of sixteen and sixty-four) being 'economically active', that is, engaged in some form of paid work. The average 'economic output' for an Edinburgh-based worker was valued at £32,697, compared to the Scottish average of £19,267. This figure is not about wages, but reflects the 'value' of an individual worker's productivity.

The biggest employer is the City of Edinburgh Council, which has more than 20,000 employees (including teachers). NHS Lothian has only slightly fewer numbers, a reflection of the high concentration of hospital and health care services in the city.

Other large employers include the Royal Bank of Scotland, Lloyds Banking Group, the University of Edinburgh, Standard Life, the Scottish Government, Aegon UK and Lothian Buses.

The largest sector of the city's economy was financial and insurance activities, accounting for almost 28 per cent of the total output. Manufacturing was the sixth largest sector, generating less than real estate activities.

BANKING AND FINANCE

Edinburgh is the second largest UK financial centre outside the City of London, and the fourth in Europe.

Cashing a cheque will rarely take place in a grander location than in the banking hall of Dundas House on St Andrew Square. The headquarters of the Royal Bank of Scotland, still a working branch, the building is topped by a huge dome painted celestial blue and pierced by 120 star-shaped windows – a stunning sight.

Before the New Town was built, the current site of Dundas House was occupied by fields and a cottage called Peace and Plenty.

The Royal Bank of Scotland, founded in 1727, is actually a relative newcomer in the Edinburgh banking world. Its rival the Bank of Scotland was formed in 1695, just one year after the creation of the Bank of England.

The Bank of Scotland originally carried out its business from very modest premises in Old Bank Close off the Lawnmarket. It moved to its present premises atop The Mound in 1806. The new building cost £75,000, the sum coming from unclaimed funds held at the bank. Bankers appropriating their customers' money? Certainly not. The structure was aggrandised into its current form in the 1860s.

One of Edinburgh's most famous unsolved murders took place on 13 November 1806. Thomas Begbie, a porter, was stabbed to death at the headquarters of the British Linen Bank in Tweedale House, off High Street. £4,392 was stolen, only a fraction of which was later recovered. The murderer has never been identified.

1814 saw the opening of the Edinburgh Savings Bank, one of first savings banks in the UK.

A bewildering variety of banks opened, closed or merged through the nineteenth century and into the post-war years. Competition was so fierce that banks always looked to find some form of commercial advantage. In 1964 the National Commercial Bank (now submerged into the Royal Bank of Scotland) opened a women-only branch on Princes Street. The same year the Bank of Scotland instituted Scotland's first American-style drive-in bank, in Corstorphine.

The activities of both the two principal banks, the Bank of Scotland and the Royal Bank, have attracted massive criticism in recent years.

But banking controversy is nothing new. John Law of Lauriston was a one-man eighteenth-century credit crunch. A gambler, serial adulterer, duellist and escaped condemned criminal, he rose to be the Controller-General of the Treasury of France, overseeing an inflationary boom based on false expectations of the value of the French colony of Louisiana. When the inevitable bust happened, Law's personal fortune dropped overnight from 10 million livres (around £65 million in today's money) to a mere 800 livres. Defrauded Parisians tried to kill him, and he died in poverty. At this point his native Edinburgh quietly forgot that they had once granted the Freedom of the City to their financial golden boy.

Bruce Marshall's 1958 novel *The Bank Audit* has the main character reflect that chartered accountants in Edinburgh were as common as pretty prostitutes in Paris: 'a good one waiting under every other lamp-post.'

POLITICS

The stone cairn on the western edge of Calton Hill was built by keepers of the vigil for a Scottish parliament, which was kept at the foot of the hill from 1992 until 1997, when Scotland voted to have its own parliament.

The new Scottish Parliament building, designed by the Spanish architect Enric Miralles, offends and delights people in equal measure. In a drama that kept Edinburgh agog and embarrassed Scots everywhere, the building finally opened in 2004, a mere three years late and costing more than ten times its original budget.

The New Observatory on Calton Hill, built in 1818, housed the Politicians Clock – so named because it has two faces.

RETAIL

Charles Jenner and Charles Kennington took a day off work to go to Musselburgh races. As a result their employer, W.R. Spence, drapers of Waterloo Place, fired them, so the two friends decided to set up on their own. In 1838 Jenners Department Store opened on Princes Street, and has been the iconic upmarket Edinburgh shopping location ever since.

PRINTING AND PUBLISHING

The first printing charter in Scotland was granted in 1507 to printer Walter Chapman (who had learned the revolutionary new trade in France) and Andrew Millar, a merchant from Edinburgh. The first book they printed was the Bible, followed by William Chaucer's *The Canterbury Tales*.

Edinburgh soon developed into a major printing centre. By 1740 there were four printing firms in the city, rising to twenty-seven companies just thirty years later. In the year 1861, more than 3,000 people were recorded as working in the printing trade in Edinburgh.

In time, well-known publishers became established – A&C Black, Constable, William Blackwood & Sons, Oliver & Boyd, Chambers, Thomas Nelson & Sons, and the mapmakers Bartholomew. Today, Edinburgh remains a publishing hub, with significant players including Birlinn, Black and White, Canongate, Edinburgh University Press, Luath and Mainstream.

The first *Encyclopaedia Britannica* was written and published in Edinburgh, issued in three volumes between 1768 and 1771 as the *Encyclopædia Britannica, or, A Dictionary of Arts and Sciences, compiled upon a New Plan*. Having undergone constant expansion and revision ever since, *Britannica* is the oldest English-language encyclopaedia still being produced, although it is no longer published in Edinburgh.

Edinburgh's pre-eminence as a centre of the printing trade saw an unusually high number of women employed in the industry, mostly in bookbinding and compositing (the setting-up of type). In 1909 there were about 800 female compositors in Edinburgh, perhaps three times the total number for the rest of the UK. The printing industry, being relatively genteel, was seen as desirable by many young working-class women (especially when compared to the alternatives, such as domestic service or laundry or shop work). Women, however, were paid less than men for the same work, and eventually the male trade unions, fearing that employers would undercut wages by relying on female labour, ensured that no further female compositors would be hired.

TOURISM

Nobody really knows how many tourists visit Edinburgh – the official total in 2010 was 3,267,000, but that figure should be taken with a pinch of salt, as many day visitors are unrecorded. Tourism generates something like £1.6 billion per year, supporting 30,000 jobs and keeping legions of men in kilts busy, even in the depths of winter.

Edinburgh is Scotland's most popular tourist destination. In 2010 the largest percentage of tourists came from Germany (13 per cent), with the USA (12 per cent) close behind, followed by France and Ireland (9 per cent each).

In the same year 2,593,577 people apparently visited the Edinburgh Festival Fringe, although that figure probably includes multiple counting, that is, one visitor going to several different events. The International Festival, meanwhile, attracted 405,392 punters (counted in the same manner). In terms of numbers, the energetic and chaotic Fringe, once literally on the edge of the official festival and dismissed as the 'lunatic fringe', has far eclipsed its 'high culture' rival.

As well as the International Festival and the Fringe, the city hosts an average of twenty-two other festivals a year, covering everything from science to storytelling.

Edinburgh's most popular paying attraction in 2010 was the castle, with 1,196,248 visitors. The most visited free attraction was the National Galleries of Scotland, which pulled in 1,281,465. The other heavyweights were, in order, St Giles Cathedral (free), the Royal Botanic Garden (free), the National Museum of Scotland (free), Edinburgh Zoo (paying), Edinburgh Bus Tours (paying) and Our Dynamic Earth (paying).

BREWING

Weak beer or ale was the preferred alternative to water in the seventeenth century, and in 1530 there were no less than 288 brewers operating in the city, many of them women known as alewives, who operated out of their apartments, yards and cellars. As brewing became more profitable, women were elbowed out. The Edinburgh Society of Brewers – men only – was established in 1596.

Brewing became a major activity in the eighteenth century, eventually graduating to the city's largest industry, with forty breweries at its height. The two giants were William Younger, who started as a brewer in Leith in 1749 and founded the Abbey and Holyrood Breweries, and William McEwan, whose Fountain Brewery was built in 1856. The Younger and McEwan brands later joined under the title Scottish & Newcastle, but when the Fountain Brewery closed in the 1990s, much of Edinburgh's historic brewing tradition vanished (along with the distinctive smell when the breweries started work for the day).

At one point Younger's Brewery made a quarter of all the beer brewed in Scotland.

Although the Caledonian Brewery on Slateford Road has undergone many changes, it still has two of the three original direct-fired brewing coppers from its founding in 1869, the last examples of this Victorian technology still in use in Britain.

PUBS, CLUBS AND BOOZE

By the year 1778 Edinburgh was home to 2,011 premises licensed for the sale of alcohol, which translated as roughly one drinking den for every 130 inhabitants.

In the same year, Edinburgh had eight licensed stills – and 400 illegal ones.

Our forebears consumed alcohol in heroic quantities, often at times we would now regard as inappropriate. In 1578 the worshippers at the Communion service of one Edinburgh church downed an astonishing 26 gallons of wine.

The oldest pub in Edinburgh may be the Sheep Heid in Duddingston, which was allegedly established in 1360, although the current building dates from the nineteenth century, when the head of a sheep or ram was indeed on display on the wall.

Sabbath-breakers – that is, those who did not attend one of the 'approved' Presbyterian churches – would be searched by Kirk Officers looking for illicit wine and food, thus preventing the sin of enjoying yourself on a Sunday. The killjoys, of course, then helped themselves to the confiscated wine at the first opportunity. Dr Alexander Pitcairn, a surgeon and Episcopalian, got round this by introducing an emetic into some of his wine. Once the bailies had spent a day throwing up violently, the good doctor was thereafter undisturbed.

Before whisky took hold, the Scottish national drink – at least for the professional classes – was claret, usually imported from France. The Napoleonic Wars saw the gradual disappearance of claret drinking. For poorer people, the preferred drink was ale.

In 1725 a tax of sixpence per barrel of malt was imposed, which would have led to a hike in the price of ale. In Glasgow, riots broke out.

In Edinburgh, opposition was more truculent, with the brewers refusing to work, thus potentially depriving a thirsty population of their daily drink. Fearing the unrest to which this would inevitably lead, the magistrates threw three brewers into prison, and broke the resistance. The tax was later reduced by 50 per cent, but the consumption of ale went into decline, while whisky became more and more popular.

The social life of professional men in eighteenth-century Edinburgh was dominated by private clubs. With no room at home for socialising – the Old Town apartments of even well-to-do residents were tiny – men met in the upper rooms of taverns, where business and pleasure intermixed, and social and professional advancement flourished over many a drink. A gentleman with enough spare coin could easily belong to half-a-dozen clubs, each of which would have a different aim or interest. Some of these clubs focused on intellectual or cultural passions, or were devoted to games and sports, though others were more singular: members of the Pious Club were punningly required to eat pies at their meetings, while the Sweating Club, the Dirty Club and the Ten Tumbler Club were devoted to drinking even more heavily than was usual for the times.

Eighteenth-century judge Lord Prestongrange was socially unpopular because he did not drink to excess. His fellow judges, who after a hard day at the circuit court were accustomed to getting tired and emotional over vast quantities of claret, were unable to conceive of a man who was near-teetotal, and thought perhaps he was simply too mean to share his wine cellar.

During the 1916 Zeppelin raid the bonded whisky warehouse of Messrs Innes and Grieves in Leith went up in flames. Whisky ran through the streets, leading to hundreds of citizens turning up with jugs, bowls and any other kind of vessel that came to hand. What could not be collected was drunk from cupped hands on the spot.

In September 1940 a distillery warehouse on Duff Street was hit by a bomb and exploded into flames. So much whisky had saturated the soil during the fire that, for many years afterwards, a warm day would make the ground round the former warehouse bloom with the overpowering scent of alcohol.

GAMBLING

General Scott of Balcomie, who had a town house on Drummond Place, was an inveterate gambler. One night he was at his usual table when a messenger brought news that the general's wife had given birth to a daughter. Scott immediately decided to win a dowry

for the girl, and doubled his usual stakes. Some hours later he was £8,000 in debt. He didn't give up, however, and at seven o'clock in the morning he departed the gambling den with £15,000. The huge sum guaranteed his daughter Henrietta's introduction to the highest echelons of society, and she went on to marry the Duke of Portland.

SWEET STUFF

The '99', the classic combination of ice-cream, cornet and Cadbury's Flake, originated at Arcari's Ice Cream Parlour, whose address was 99 Portobello High Street.

In the early nineteenth century High School Wynd was home to what was called the Jib House, where the pupils would avidly purchase a home-made sweet called 'jib' or 'jube'. Invented by a Frenchman, the jube consisted of two parts treacle and one part sugar boiled together. The schoolboys then had the choice of flavouring the soft sweet with either ground ginger or a variety of spices, the latter applied not directly but through rubbing the jube with the cork of the selected spice bottle.

In 1892 Alexander Grant of McVitie & Price, bakers of Edinburgh, created the recipe for what became known as McVitie's Digestive Biscuits, still one of the most popular biscuits in the country. The name referred to the belief that the ingredients would assist digestion for those with weak stomachs.

TEA AND COFFEE

In 1742 Duncan Forbes, later Lord President of the Court of Session, denounced 'the villainous practice' of drinking 'that abominable drug'. He was referring to tea. His Lordship proposed banning the substance for the majority of the population, exempting only the upper classes, who would be allowed to indulge only if they paid an annual poll tax.

The first coffee house opened in the city in 1677, although it quickly closed when an 'unlawful' preacher was caught giving a sermon on the premises at the same time as divine service in the approved churches. The owner of the establishment was fined 500 merks.

By 1680 Edinburgh's movers and shakers were gathering in coffee houses to read and discuss the gazettes and newspapers that were arriving from London. This freedom of information terrified the authorities, and soon all coffee house owners were obliged to pay a huge bond that would be forfeited if they allowed unapproved newspapers to be read in their establishments. Anything that arrived from London, or was printed elsewhere, had first to be handed over to state officials for censorship.

These episodes show that, although coffee was certainly drunk at coffee houses, that was not the main purpose. Essentially coffee houses were social spaces where a broad range of activities could take place with more elbow-room than elsewhere. Even the most well-heeled dweller of the Old Town tenements rarely had more than three rooms in his apartment, and so everyone from lawyers and writers to merchants and bankers used coffee houses as their offices. Coffee houses were an essential part of the social and business fabric of Edinburgh. As water was often unsafe to drink, the choice was between coffee and alcohol, the former usually being the choice before lunch.

Is tea the Devil's brew? In 1726 Alexander Pennecuik's *A Lecture to the Ladies* stated that Edinburgh ladies who drank tea were perpetuating the sin of Eve in the Garden of Eden:

'Was't not enough to taste the damning Tree
But you must guzzle down that cursed *Tea*.'

Even worse, tea was actually demonic in nature:

'A Plant which in the Devil's Garden grew
By which a second Time he poisons you.'

Milk and sugar, Mr Pennecuik?

BIBLIOGRAPHY

Arnot, Hugo, *The History of Edinburgh, from the Earliest Accounts, to the Year 1780* (Thomas Turnball; Edinburgh, 1816)

Atkinson, Kate, *One Good Turn* (Black Swan; London, 2007)

Atkinson, Kate, *When Will There Be Good News?* (Black Swan; London, 2008)

Banks, Iain, *The Bridge* (Macmillan; London, 1986)

Banks, Iain, *Complicity* (Little, Brown & Co.; London, 1993)

Black, Tony, *Truth Lies Bleeding* (Arrow; London, 2011)

Black, Tony, *Murder Mile* (Arrow; London, 2012)

Bondeson, Jan, *Greyfriars Bobby – The Most Faithful Dog in the World* (Amberley; Stroud, 2011)

Broughton History Society Newsletter, No. 26, Winter 2009/10

Bruce, David, *Scotland The Movie* (Polygon; Edinburgh, 1996)

Cadell, Patrick, *The Iron Mills of Cramond* (Bratton Publishing/ University of Edinburgh; Edinburgh, 1973)

Carr, Caleb, *The Italian Secretary* (Little, Brown; London, 2005)

Chambers, Robert, *The Domestic Annals of Scotland* (W & R Chambers; Edinburgh and London, 1858)

Chambers, Robert, *Traditions of Edinburgh* (W & R Chambers; Edinburgh, 1868)

City of Edinburgh Council, *Edinburgh by Numbers 2012/13* (Economic Development Committee; The City of Edinburgh Council, 2012)

City of Edinburgh Council, *River Flow and Flooding* (City of Edinburgh Council; 2007)

City of Edinburgh Council, *Survey of Gardens and Designed Landscapes Summary Report* (City Development Department; City of Edinburgh Council, 2009)

City of Edinburgh Council, *City of Edinburgh Report on the Evolution and Development of Public Health Administration* (Edinburgh City Council; Edinburgh, n.d.)

Colston, James, *The Edinburgh and District Water Supply* (Colston & Co.; Edinburgh, 1890)

Daniel, William S., *History of the Abbey and Palace of Holyrood* (Duncan Anderson; Edinburgh, 1852)

Dixon, Norman, *The Placenames of Midlothian* (unpublished PhD thesis, University of Edinburgh, 1947)

Douglas, David, *Early Travellers In Scotland* (James Maclehose & Sons; Glasgow, 1891)

Dudley Edwards, Owen, and Graham Richardson (eds.), *Edinburgh* (Canongate; Edinburgh, 1983)

Dunlop, Eileen and Anthony Kamm (eds.) *A Book of Old Edinburgh* (MacDonald Publishers; Edinburgh, 1983)

Edinburgh Airport, *Climate Change Adaptation Plan for Edinburgh Airport* (Edinburgh Airport; 2011)

Fife, Malcolm, *The Nor Loch – Scotland's Lost Loch* (Scotforth Books; Lancaster, 2004)

Foster, Allan, *The Literary Traveller in Edinburgh* (Mainstream Publishing; Edinburgh, 2005)

Galbraith, Gillian, *Blood in the Water* (Mercat Press; Edinburgh, 2007)

Geikie, Sir Archibald, *Scottish Reminiscences* (James Maclehose and Sons; Glasgow, 1904)

Gillies, J.B., *Edinburgh Past and Present* (Oliphant, Anderson & Ferrier; Edinburgh, 1886)

Gillon, Jack, City of Edinburgh Council and Dawn McDowell, *Edinburgh's Post-War Listed Buildings* (City of Edinburgh Council/ Historic Scotland; Edinburgh, 2010)

Gordon, Eleanor and Esther Breitenbach (eds.), *The World is Ill Divided: Women's work in Scotland in the Nineteenth and Twentieth Centuries* (Edinburgh University Press; Edinburgh, 1990)

Gowans, James, *Edinburgh in the Days of our Grandfathers* (John C. Nimmo; London, 1886)

Grant, James, *Old and New Edinburgh: its history, its people and its places* (Cassell; London, 1887)

Groome, Frances H. (ed.) *Ordnance Gazetteer of Scotland: A Survey of Scottish Topography, Statistical, Biographical and Historical* (Grange Publishing Works; Edinburgh, 1882-1885)

Haggart, David, *The Life of David Haggart, alias John Wilson, alias John Morison, alias Barney McCoul, alias John McColgan, alias Daniel O'Brien, alias The Switcher* (W. and C. Tait; Edinburgh, 1821)

Harris, Stuart, *The Place Names of Edinburgh* (Steve Savage; Edinburgh, 2002)

Haswell-Smith, Hamish, *The Scottish Islands* (Canongate; Edinburgh, 1996)

Hendrie, William F., *Discovering the River Forth* (John Donald Publishers; Edinburgh, 1996)

Hendrie, William F., *The Forth at War* (Birlinn; Edinburgh, 2005)

Hume Brown, Peter, *History of Scotland from the Revolution of 1689 to the Disruption, 1843* (Cambridge University Press; Cambridge, 1911)

Hunter, D.L.G., *Edinburgh Tramways Album* (Turntable Publications; Sheffield, 1974)

Jardine, Quentin, *Skinner's Rules* (Headline; London, 2009)

Jardine, Quentin, *The Loner* (Headline; London, 2011)

Jeffrey, Andrew, *This Present Emergency: Edinburgh, the River Forth and South-East Scotland and the Second World War* (Mainstream; Edinburgh & London, 1992)

Johnston, James B., *Place-Names of Scotland* (James Maclehose & Sons; Glasgow, 1892)

Johnston, Paul, *Body Politic* (1998), *The Bone Yard* (1999), *Water of Death* (1999), *The Blood Tree* (2000), *The House of Dust* (2002) (all Hodder & Stoughton; London)

Jones, Richard, *History & Mystery Walks: Edinburgh* (AA Publishing; Basingstoke, 2009)

Kielty, Martin *Big Noise: The Sound of Scotland* (Black & White Publishing; Edinburgh, 2006)

Kisling, Vernon K. (ed.), *Zoo and Aquarium History: Ancient Animal Collections to Zoological Gardens* (CRC Press; Boca Raton, Florida, 2001)

Knight, Alanna, *Enter Second Murderer* (Macmillan; London, 2005)

Kolb, Hugh H., "Factors Affecting the Movements of Dog Foxes in Edinburgh" in *The Journal of Applied Ecology* Vol. 21, 1984

Lindsay, Robert, *The Historie and Chronicles of Scotland, 1436–1565* (Baskett & Co.; Edinburgh, 1728)

Linklater, Eric, *Edinburgh* (Newnes; London, 1960)

Littlejohn, H. D., *Report on the Sanitary Conditions of the City of Edinburgh* (The City Council; Edinburgh, 1865)

Lownie, Andrew, *The Literary Companion to Edinburgh* (Methuen; London, 2000)

McCall Smith, Alexander, *The Sunday Philosophy Club* (Little, Brown; London, 2004)

McDairmid, Hugh, *Scottish Eccentrics* (George Routledge & Sons; London, 1936)

McGowan, John, *Policing the Metropolis of Scotland. A History of the Police and Systems of Police in Edinburgh & Edinburghshire, 1770-1833* (Turlough Publishers; Musselburgh, 2012)

McLevy, James (ed. George Scott-Moncrieff), *The Casebook of a Victorian Detective* (Canongate; Edinburgh, 1975)

Massey, Alison, *The Edinburgh and Glasgow Union Canal* (Falkirk Museums; Falkirk, 1983)

Massie, Allan, *Edinburgh* (Sinclair-Stevenson; London, 1994)

Massie, Allan (ed.), *Edinburgh & The Borders in Verse* (Secker & Warburg; London, 1983)

Masson, David, *Edinburgh Sketches & Memories* (Adam and Charles Black; London and Edinburgh, 1892)

Maxwell, Herbert, *Edinburgh: A Historical Study* (Williams & Norgate; London, 1916)

Milne, John, *Gaelic Place Names of the Lothians* (Mcdougall's Educational Company; London and Edinburgh, 1912)

Mullay, Sandy, *The Edinburgh Encyclopedia* (Mainstream; Edinburgh & London, 1996)

Nimmo, Ian, *Edinburgh The New Town* (John Donald; Edinburgh, 1991)

Paton, James (ed.), *Scottish History & Life* (James Maclehose & Sons; Edinburgh, 1902)

Ramsay, Dean, *Reminiscences of Scottish Life & Character* (T. K. Foulis; Edinburgh, 1908)

Rodger, Donald, Jon Stokes and James Ogilvie, *Heritage Trees of Scotland* (Forestry Commission Scotland; Edinburgh, 2006)

Richardson, Ralph, "On the earthquake shocks experienced in the Edinburgh district on Friday, January 18, 1889" in *The Scottish Geographical Magazine* Vol. 5. No. 3, 1889

Ruckley, Brian, *The Edinburgh Dead* (Orbit; London, 2010)

Russell, John, *The Story of Leith* (Thomas Nelson; London & Edinburgh, 1922)

Scott-Moncrieff, George, *Edinburgh* (Oliver & Boyd; Edinburgh & London, 3rd edition, 1964)

The Scottish Historical Review Vol. 3 (1906) and Vol. 9 (1912)

Shepherd, Thomas H., *Modern Athens, displayed in a series of views, or Edinburgh in the Nineteenth Century* (Jones & Co., London, 1829)

Smeaton, Oliphant, *Edinburgh and its Story* (J.M. Dent & Co.; London, 1904)

Stark, J., *The Picture of Edinburgh: Containing a Description of the City and its Environs* (John Fairburn/Manners and Miller/John Anderson; Edinburgh, 1825)

Stevenson, Robert Louis, *Edinburgh: Picturesque Notes* (Seeley & Co.; London, 1903)

Taylor, Les, *Luftwaffe over Scotland* (Whittles Publishing; Dunbeath, 2010)

Telfer, Hamish McDonald, *The Origins, Governance and Social Structure of Club Cross Country Running in Scotland, 1885 – 1914* (PhD thesis, Faculty of Management, Department of Sports Studies; University of Stirling, 2006)

Thomson, John, *The Edinburgh Town Guard: the story of the capital's first police force* (Monty Books; Edinburgh, 2001)

Topham, Edward, *Letters from Edinburgh: written in the years 1774 and 1775: containing some observations on the diversions, customs, manners, and laws, of the Scotch nation, during a six months residence in Edinburgh* (J. Dodsley; London, 1776)

Urquhart, Fred, *The Ferret Was Abraham's Daughter* (Methuen; London, 1949)

Urquhart, Fred, *Jezebel's Dust* (Methuen; London, 1951)

Walker, Patrick, *Biographia Presbyteriana* (D. Speare & J. Stevenson; Edinburgh, 1827)

Watt, Francis, *Terrors of the law; being the portraits of three lawyers, Bloody Jeffreys, The bluidy advocate Mackenzie, the original Weir of Hermiston* (J. Lane; London and New York, 1902)

Watt, Francis, *Edinburgh and The Lothians* (Methuen; London, 1912)

Watt, Francis, *The Book of Edinburgh Anecdote* (T.N. Foulis; London & Edinburgh, 1913)

Wham, Alasdair, *Edinburgh and Lothians – Exploring the Lost Railways* (GC Books; Wigtown, 2006)

Williamson, M.G., *Edinburgh: A Historical and Topographical Account of the City* (Methuen; London, 1906)

Wilson, Daniel, *Memorials of Edinburgh in the Olden Time* (Thomas C. Jack; Edinburgh, 1886)

Plus hundreds of newspaper stories, websites, leaflets and tourist brochures.